Renovating Furniture

Contents

Introduction

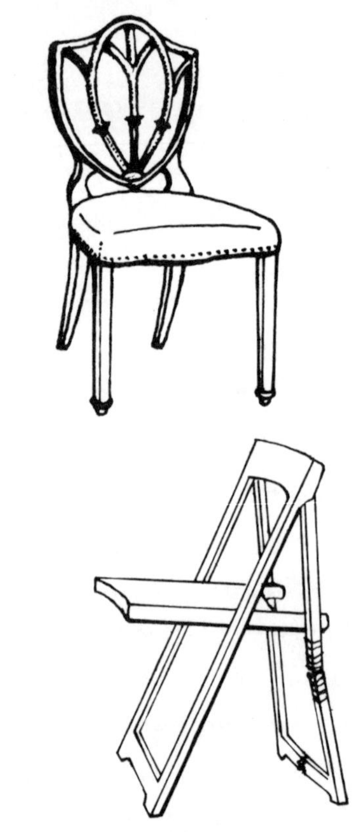

Renovation or repair can transform shabby or broken chairs

The cost of new furniture has increased five or six times since the end of the war. A genuine antique may have increased fifty-fold in value. Even items made between the wars now have a sales value far in excess of their intrinsic worth. Cabinets, chests of drawers, even hard chairs, which a short time ago would have ended up in a junk shop or on a rubbish tip now find eager buyers who are prepared to renovate and repair them, not only to save money, but because the wood is more seasoned and of better quality than that used in many of today's pieces.

Furniture is subject to hard wear. Deterioration and damage in the average household are inevitable, but there is no need to make do with a shabby table or a cupboard with ill-fitting doors, still less to replace them with something new and probably expensive, before considering a simple repair.

It is always advisable, however, to consider whether a repair is justified, or whether it is prejudicial to its worth. A really old and good-quality piece, even if scratched and chipped, will probably be spoiled if the surface is stripped down and a veneer or synthetic polish put on it. Any attempt to disguise the consequences of great age is to be regretted. An antique may not be strong enough to withstand daily use, but it probably has its place as a treasured show piece, and anyway it has a sales value to a professional renovator who will know just how far renovation should go.

But the majority of broken, damaged and deteriorating pieces are essentially utilitarian, subject to hard daily use. The main object is to ensure that they are strong and attractive to look at. For these pieces a few hours' work can transform them, prolonging their useful life and saving the modest cost of materials used in renovation over and over. Two objectives should be kept in mind: first to ensure that the repair restores the strength and function of the furniture, and second to ensure that everything that is done is so unnoticeable that the observer is unaware that the original blemish-free appearance has had to be largely restored or replaced.

Simple repair work on other

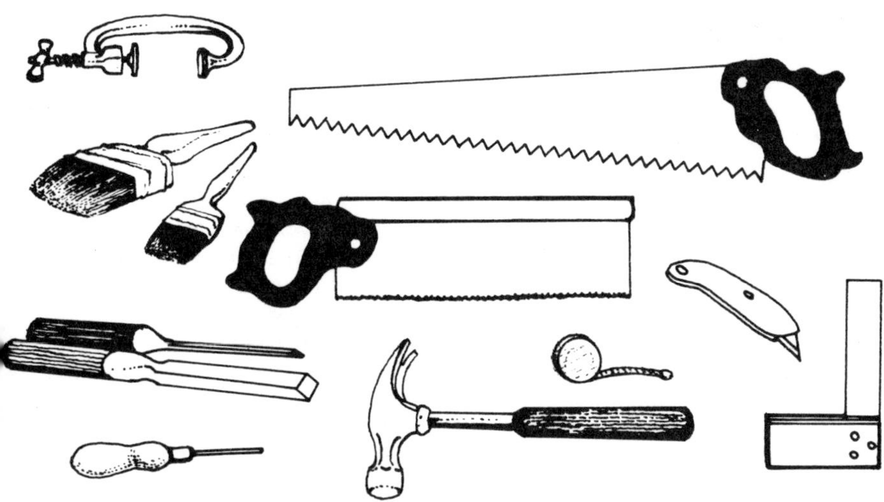

Essential tools make work better and easier

people's rejected pieces of furniture can provide you with much needed items. At auction sales there are often lots covering the residue of the sale – collections of so-called junk items of little interest to dealers. Such old and broken pieces are taken in part-exchange by furniture dealers, or sometimes simply because the customer says that he will buy new furniture only if the dealer takes away the old stuff.

Many dealers burn some of these items because it is cheaper than paying the local authority to take them to a rubbish tip. Simple items, such as kitchen chairs, children's cots and small tables can be picked up for the proverbial song. They will be dirty and probably damaged, but for literally pence spent on repair and cleaning pounds can be saved.

For this interesting and not very taxing work – one is justified in calling it a hobby for a winter's evening or a leisurely weekend – good quality tools and equipment can make all the difference between a satisfying repair and an amateurish, make-do job.

In the following pages a few special tools and materials for unusual projects are mentioned in the description of a particular work. But for the general run of tasks the following are really essential:

Adhesive tape – gummed brown paper, cellulose.
Bradawl for making guide holes.
Chisels, at least two sizes.
Cramps.
Drill and set of bits.
Glasspaper – coarse, medium, and extra supplies of fine grade.
Hammer.
Knives – including the craft type with detachable blades.
Paint brushes.
Rules – steel straight edge, flexible tape.
Saws – tenon and panel.
Screwdrivers.
Steel wool – fine grade.
Try square for checking right angles.
Wooden mallet.

Materials

As regards materials it is better to buy as you prepare for a particular repair. Paints, spirits, adhesives, etc., which may deteriorate once the container is opened and the contents partially used, are best bought in the smallest quantity applicable for the job. This will avoid waste, as well as disappointment when tackling another repair months later.

It would be wrong to under-rate the advances made by manufacturers to cope with the demand of do-it-yourself enthusiasts. The aim is usually to make an allegedly tiresome job easier, quicker, and provide a better result. However, the craft of furniture making is an old one and its members discovered near-perfect techniques a long time ago.

Many of the materials used in manufacture and repair have stood the test of time, and cannot really be bettered, even if they sometimes involve more and slower work.

Generally speaking, it is a virtue to be a little old-fashioned in one's approach, and the shop salesman's claim that a new product is 'as good as' or 'better than' needs proof in an example of the results.

The basic materials required for the general run of furniture repairs and renovations are as follows:

Bleach – domestic type.
Fillers – usually based on plaster of Paris.
Insecticide, for woodworm.
Methylated spirit.
Paints – gloss, matt, enamel, aerosol.
Panel pins, various sizes.
Plastic wood in different shades.
Polishes – french, polyurethane, wax.
Screws – various sizes, and preferably in a brass or chromium finish.
Stains – water and oil.
Stripper.
Turpentine and turpentine substitute (white spirit).
Varnishes – clear and coloured.

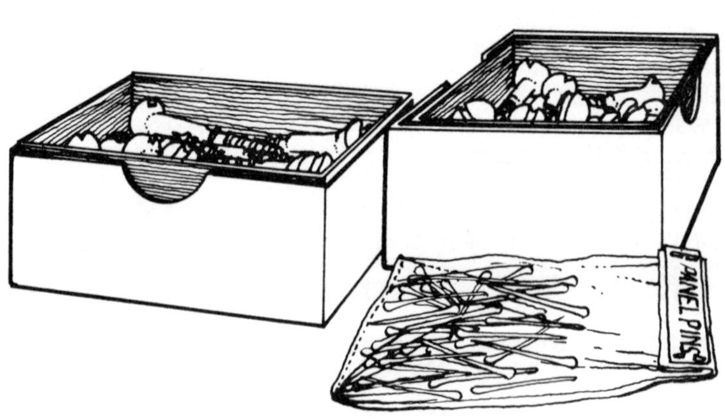

Screws and panel pins are cheaper if bought in quantity

TURPS
red
PLASTIC

Types of furniture wood

Before attempting any renovation or repair to a dingy, shabby piece of furniture, try to identify the wood. Layers of varnish, and possibly paint, may be concealing attractive wood, especially if the furniture is fairly old. If it is modern it has probably been covered with a veneer, which presents a more difficult problem in making any change in the appearance of the surface.

Generally speaking, good furniture is made from hardwoods, with one exception: Douglas fir, which is a golden brown softwood, has in recent years been quite widely used for modern items. It has a tendency to split.

Furniture hardwoods

Afrormosia, a richly-coloured African timber, used only in costly furniture.

Ash, white or cream, often used in plywood and veneers.

Beech, an almost white wood widely used in chairs.

Elm, used mostly for outdoor items, but occasionally for robust pieces such as linen chests and plant containers.

Japanese ash, a pale cream timber, used for light articles of fairly fragile design.

Mahogany, originating in sub-tropical areas of Africa and the Americas, has a distinctive rich red-brown colour. Many modern items are covered with a mahogany veneer.

Oak, light brown or beige, originates from England, Japan, Europe and the USA. It is used only in heavy, robust pieces with a minimum of decorative work. A characteristic is the sheen of silver flecks. Time changes its colour from light to dark.

Obeche, an African timber widely used in plywood and for so-called white-wood items for kitchens and bedrooms.

Rosewood, from Central America and Indonesia, is regarded by many as the most beautiful of all furniture woods. A purple-brown timber, it can be finished to a perfect gloss and needs no polish. As it is very expensive all but the most costly items are merely covered with a rosewood veneer.

Teak, a red-brown wood from India, is heavy and oily. It is sometimes used for furniture, but in the average home will be found as block flooring, draining boards, or as garden furniture.

Walnut, a medium-brown wood with attractive graining, grows all over the world. It was greatly favoured by the masters of English furniture design in the eighteenth and nineteenth centuries. Unfortunately, English walnut (the most beautifully grained) is now too expensive except for veneers.

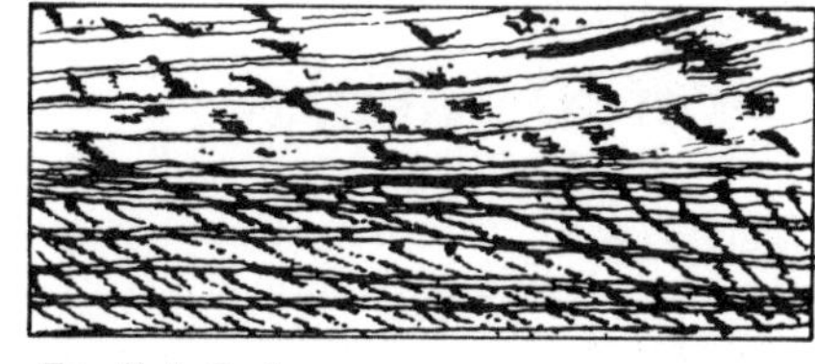

English Oak

Walnut

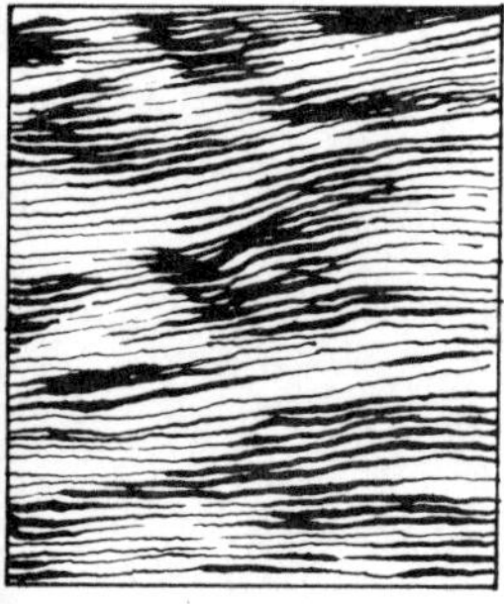

African Mahogany

Ash

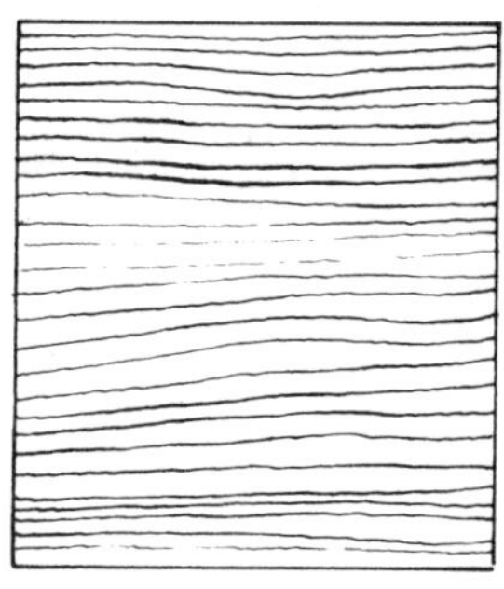

Douglas Fir

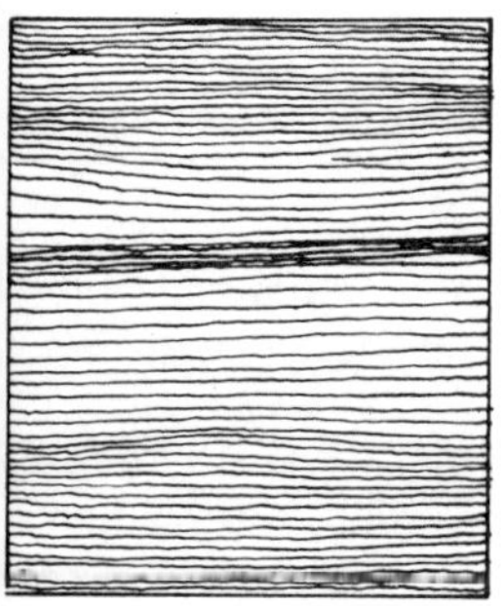

Red Cedar

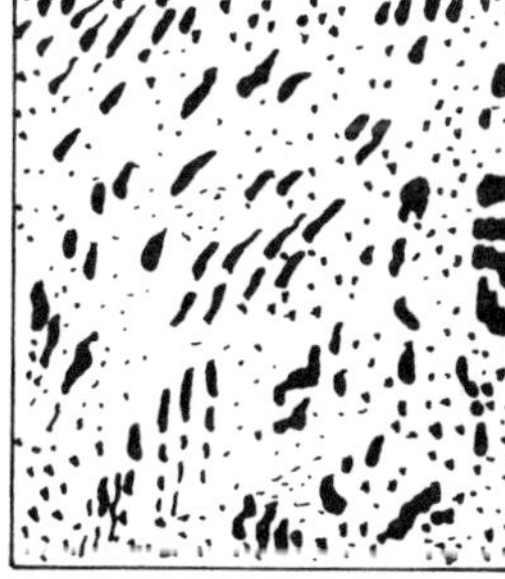

Beech

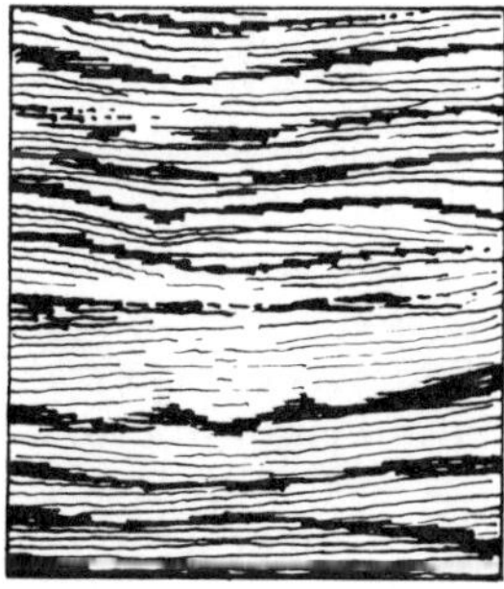

Teak

The different grains of various types of wood

Dealing with blemishes

Bruises

Veneered surfaces are prone to bruising through heavy or angular objects coming into violent contact. The only feasible remedy is to prick some holes in the dent with a fine needle, cover with a damp cloth and rub with a hot iron in order to make the wood swell. It is, however, rather a risky business as the steam may dissolve the glue and loosen the veneer.

The method works better with solid wood. In this case, of course, there is no point in pricking the area but wax polish should be removed to enable the steam to reach the wood fibres.

Burns

Usually burn marks on furniture come from cigarettes. Due to the presence of polish the burn may have penetrated well below the surface. All charred wood should be removed by rubbing vigorously in a circular motion with a tiny ball of steel wool. Plastic wood is the best filler. With the appropriate stain for the wood, experiment with varying amounts of stain in trial lumps of plastic wood until you are satisfied that you have a reasonably good match. Press in with the fingers to achieve a level slightly above that of the surrounding wood. Rub level with glasspaper and then rub in a little linseed oil. When dry wipe away any surplus and, if the patch is still obvious, brush on a little stain. A final treatment with a coloured wax polish to the whole area should produce a satisfactory result.

Cracks

Small cracks can be filled with stopping, available under various trade names and in the colours of the principal furniture woods. You can make your own with beeswax, rosin, shellac and powdered pigment of the desired colour. The beeswax is shredded in a small receptacle and a little rosin and shellac is mixed with it; then melt the ingredients by placing the container in very hot water. *Do not* attempt to melt them over a gas flame or electric element.

Carefully pour the mixture into the crack while still warm and fluid; the amount sufficient for the stopping should come slightly above the level of the surrounding wood. When dry and hard rub down and polish.

Home-made stopping is ideal for filling cracks and scratches

Scratches

Proprietary scratch removers are simply stains in a bottle with an applicator. Any wood stain which is a good matching colour will be effective if applied carefully with a fine paint brush. A wax crayon, if the right shade can be obtained, is good for deeper scratches so long as the area is then protected with a silicone wax polish. On dark wood iodine, applied with an artist's paint brush, can be a quick and simple remedy.

Heat marks

The light stains left by hot utensils on polished surfaces are best treated by first cleaning the area with methylated spirit to remove the wax finish and then rubbing in a light or dark tan shoe polish; apply the polish a little at a time and rub well before repeating the process until the right shade is obtained. Thereafter apply a wax polish to the whole area.

If the surface has been lacquered with polyurethane, however, methylated spirit will not remove the lacquer, and the only solution is to rub it away with fine steel wool; then stain and re-lacquer.

Stains

Heavy grease stains, notably from candles, should first be hardened by placing a polythene bag containing ice cubes on the area and leaving it till the ice has melted. Some of the excess grease can then be shifted with the rounded end of a nail file, held almost horizontally. Next lay two thicknesses of blotting paper over the mark and rub with a hot iron.

With veneered surfaces the iron should be below the lowest temperature, ie, unplugged before use.

Ink stains respond to a quick and restrained brushing with household bleach, washing the surface immediately the stain fades. Several applications of bleach may be necessary, but washing it away is essential each time to prevent the surrounding area being too badly affected. A little rubbing with glasspaper and staining completes the job.

Stains from wines and spirits are virtually permanent unless washed off immediately, as alcohol will dissolve and change the colour of most finishes. The visible damage can sometimes be minimised by rubbing in some linseed oil, allowing it to dry, and then repolishing. But complete eradication almost certainly means removing the surface of the whole area with steel wool and glasspaper and refinishing.

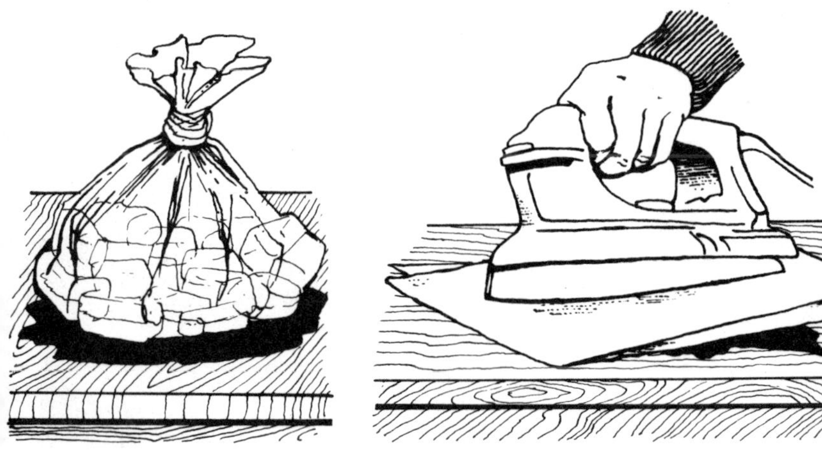

Cold and hot treatments to remove grease marks

Finishes, old and new

Modern waxes and silicone-based polishes are designed to be long-lasting and are therefore quite difficult to remove. Equally, varnishes (and paints) will require effort to get rid of them before refinishing a piece of furniture.

Removing the old finish

Burning off a finish with a blow lamp, however effective on doors, window frames and other robust parts of the house, is not advisable in the case of furniture. Damage to the surface is almost inevitable, and glue in joints will be destroyed.

Chemical strippers, either in liquid or paste form, are completley effective, though somewhat messy, and all traces of them must be washed away with warm water or methylated spirit. If it is necessary to add detergent to the water to remove any signs of grease or vestiges of polish, this must also be rinsed away with pure water. At all stages of removing the stripper and the debris, be reticent with the amount of water: wring out the sponge or cloth before each small area is cleaned rather than dousing the furniture with copious amounts of water which will rapidly soak into the porous surface and which will take hours to dry.

Always bear in mind that these strippers can injure the skin and are toxic. Wear rubber gloves, work in airy conditions, keep children out of the way, and thoroughly clean or destroy all articles used during the work.

If the finish is old or if varnish or paint has been badly applied by an amateur two or more applications of

Always wear protective gloves when using paint and varnish strippers

stripper may be necessary. If some of the original finish remains after washing leave the job until the next day and apply more stripper to those areas.

Some words of warning. Inlays, marquetry, and small carvings are usually glued to the wood. Stripper may loosen them or split them. Keep the application of stripper on such parts to the minimum to be effective and remove it as soon as bubbles appear. If the decorative section is extremely delicate it may be safer not to use stripper at the edges, but to work patiently with steel wool and fine glasspaper.

Types of new finish

With the old finish removed there comes the decision on the new one. The main choices are to bleach, to stain, to varnish or to french polish.

Bleaching

Bleaching is attractive if the wood is naturally light in colour, such as beech. It also has its points if the original stain has left patches of dark colour or if the stripper has itself caused some staining. But do not be too determined to remove all light and shade. The surface of natural wood is rarely perfectly even in hue. Domestic bleach, undiluted and brushed on is usually effective. Hydrogen peroxide is also good. Both these liquids are strong and can be injurious to the skin, so wear rubber gloves, work in the open air or near an open window, and be sure to rinse away with cold water and leave in a current of fresh air to dry.

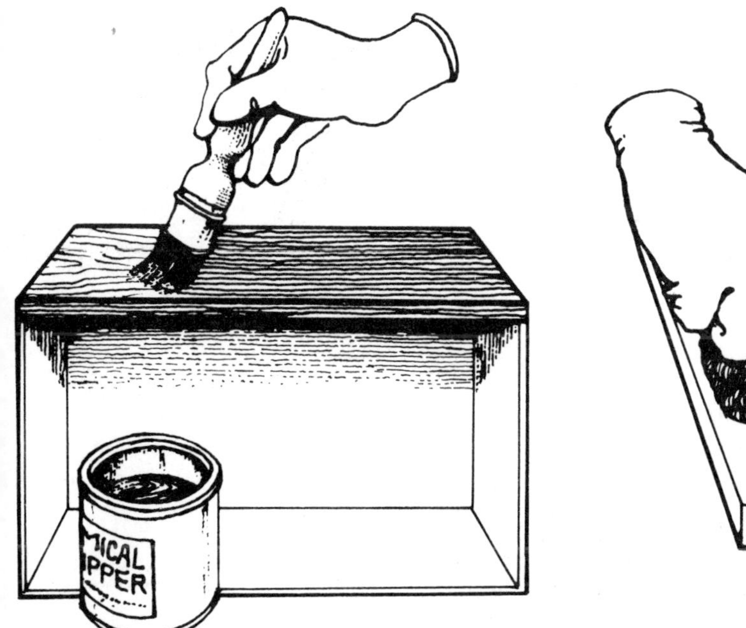

Apply stripper to one area at a time, and rinse before starting on another section.

Steel wool will remove paint or varnish from awkward places

Finishes, old and new

Staining

Wood stains are of three kinds: spirit, water and oil. Spirit stain has the property of strong penetration through the surface of the wood, but it is not easy to achieve a uniformly even colour because of the way it instantly soaks into the wood, and the amount on the brush will always affect the hue. It is wise to experiment on another piece of wood in order to get the knack of charging the brush little and often and working rapidly.

Water stains are more easily applied if you work quickly and do not attempt to soak any area. The stain will penetrate quite quickly and the first appearance will be different from that a few minutes later. It is wise to dissolve the stain in fairly hot water to assist penetration, though this may raise the grain, necessitating some light glasspapering after the wood is dry.

Oil stains are usually dyes dissolved in turpentine and some petrol derivative. They penetrate well and will not fade. Their disadvantage is that they tend to soak more readily into the softer areas of the wood and may therefore cause a marked variation in colour. The trouble can be avoided by having a clean, non-fluffy cloth handy to wipe away any newly

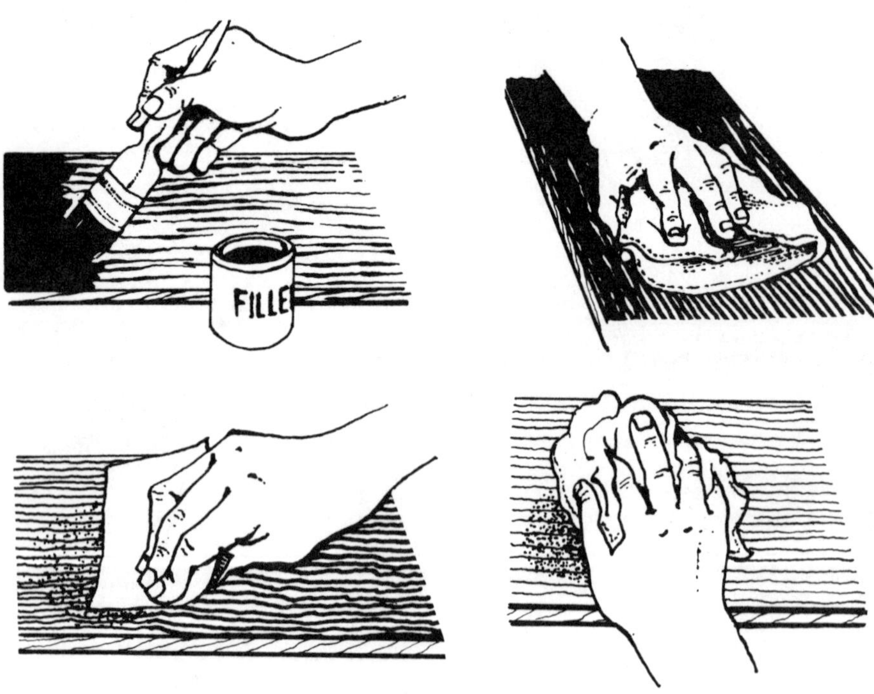

Apply filler liberally along the grain. When almost dry wipe away excess across the grain

applied stain which is apparently producing a darker colour than the rest of the wood being treated.

Varnish

The result of stripping and staining may be depressing at first glance, because the smooth glossy finish has gone. The next step depends on the type of wood – whether it is close-grained or open-grained.

Close-grained woods are ash, birch, cherry, elm, maple, yellow pine which are hard; and cypress, fir, spruce, sugar pine and white pine which are soft.

Open-grained woods are chestnut, mahogany, oak, rosewood and walnut and are all hard.

The only close-grained woods which may need a filler are ash, elm and maple. All open-grained woods need it in order to get a smooth surface. Ready-mixed fillers in light, medium and dark shades of most woods are easy to use.

The filler, which can usually be thinned if necessary to a creamy consistency with a little turpentine or white spirit, is applied with a fairly stiff brush, always in the direction of the grain. Wipe off any excess after about ten minutes with a lint-free cloth, wiping across the grain so as to prevent removing the filler from the crevices. Leave for twenty-four hours to dry thoroughly and then rub along the grain with fine glasspaper until the surface is perfectly smooth. Wipe off all the dust.

You have a variety of choices for finishing; the purpose of them all is not only to enhance the appearance but to seal the surface. Probably the most popular for the amateur are the synthetic lacquers, usually polyurethanes. They are available in matt, satin and gloss finishes. The most useful are transparent, though it is possible to obtain them in shades which match the wood concerned, but it is rather pointless to use them on wood you have already stained, and as more than one coat of lacquer will be applied it is almost inevitable that the shade will end up darker than that desired.

Polyurethanes are very hard-wearing, resistant to water and heat, and produce a high gloss – some people would say unnaturally high. But for table tops and anything liable to suffer hard knocks these lacquers are probably unparalleled.

Lacquers should be brushed on a little at a time with rapid strokes. Allow to dry, rub over with a ball of steel wool, brush away all debris, and apply another coat. Repeat the process for a third coat.

Waxing

Waxing may be preferred as it gives a rather richer-looking finish than the synthetic lacquers. The wood must first of all be treated with a sealer or oil. Sealers are either based on shellac or polyurethane. Two or three thin coats should be applied, the final one rubbed down after it is dry with fine glasspaper to provide a key for the wax polish.

Waxing is easier with modern liquids but really there is nothing to match the solid polishes made from beeswax and turpentine – and the white waxes, not those purporting to match woods. Apply the polish in a thin layer and work into the surface with wire wool, rubbing quite lightly and with a circular motion. Repeat at least three times, finally finishing off with a lint-free duster.

Finishes, old and new

Oiling

An oiled finish is not so popular these days, but is very attractive for heavy pieces which are either genuine or imitation antiques. Oiled surfaces have a rich matt finish, in contrast to the shiny appearance loved by advertisers of polishes.

The best oil to use is boiled linseed, though there are branded oils which are quite good, if rather more expensive than linseed, obtainable from old-fashioned hardware stores. Linseed oil tends to darken wood but this effect can be minimised a little by diluting it with turpentine substitute in the proportion of one part of turps to three parts of oil.

Apply the oil with a soft brush or sponge, working rapidly so that patchiness does not occur. Be economical with the amount of oil, applying three coats with time in between to allow the oil to soak in and dry, the interval depending on the atmosphere, but even in dry warm conditions eight hours should be the minimum.

After the third application, which will probably take longer to dry and indicates that the wood has absorbed all it can, wipe away any surplus with a lint-free duster. You can leave the surface as it is or protect it with wax polish. In the latter case apply as for waxing.

French polish

The best finish is, of course, french polish. There is an aura of mystery about the process, inferring that only an experienced and trained craftsman can produce the unique sheen which was the usual one on small pieces of furniture, both cheap and expensive, a century ago. In fact the secret for success is to use the right material with patient application.

Disappointing results are invariably due to using the wrong french polish. There are six principal polishes, each of them suitable for a particular wood.

General french polish, composed of methylated spirit and orange shellac, is suitable chiefly for floors and unimportant pieces of furniture. It is cheaper than others, but does not give a brilliant appearance and often produces a yellowish tinge.

Button polish, methylated spirit and button shellac, gives a light or medium colour to mahogany, light to medium colour to oak, medium to dark colour on walnut.

White polish, methylated spirit and white shellac, is for natural oak and light walnut.

Garnet polish, methylated spirit and garnet shellac, gives a dark warm finish to oak, mahogany and walnut.

Red polish, methylated spirit, garnet shellac, and bismarck brown, gives a dark red finish to rosewood.

Black polish, methylated spirit, garnet shellac and spirit black, is the finish for ebony.

Brush polish, the nearest to a universal french polish, may be used on plywood which has been stained to simulate a particular hardwood. As the name suggests, it is brushed on, to fill the grain. After it has hardened it is rubbed down with fine glasspaper and then another coat of garnet polish is applied.

But for all worthwhile french polishing jobs on hardwoods the appropriate polish should be used. Any first class DIY shop will stock the type desired or make it up for you.

It is assumed that the surface to be polished has been treated with filler, stain, etc. First rub down well with fine glasspaper to achieve a perfectly smooth finish. Remove all dust.

Make a 'rubber' from a wad of cotton wool about 15cm square and 3cm thick. Fold in half. Fold the corners of the doubled edge to the centre to make a triangle. Place on a piece of non-fluffy linen or cotton rag about 20cm square. Bring back the corners of the rag and twist together over the base of the triangle of cotton wool to produce a rubber which is roughly in the shape of a foot, the twisted ends providing a grip at the 'ankle'.

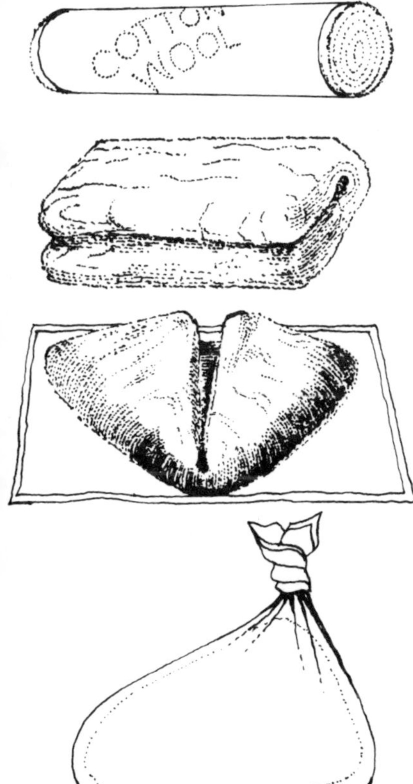

Method of making a rubber for French polishing

As polish must be applied sparingly it is a good idea to pierce the cork or stopper on the bottle with a small hole so that the polish may be shaken out, a few drops at a time, on to the cotton wool temporarily removed from its protective rag (never directly on to the exterior of the rag). Replace the rag and begin polishing with a firm movement up and down the grain. When the surface has become slightly glossy leave the job for two or three hours till completely dry.

Take two pieces of fine glasspaper and rub the faces together to blunt the cutting granules. Wipe a little linseed oil over the paper and rub away any gloss on the wood. Re-charge the cotton wool with polish, smear a little linseed oil on the pad cover and begin polishing with a circular motion, being careful not to lift the rubber until the whole area has been treated.

The process will have to be repeated two, three, or more times until the surface is even in appearance, though still quite dull.

The final job is to renew the cotton wool, sprinkle just a few drops of polish on it, replace the rag, and rub with straight strokes along the grain.

Gradually the oily sheen will disappear, the shellac will be hardened by exposure to the air and by friction, and the characteristic sheen of french polishing will be your reward for quite hard work. If the appearance is not up to expectations it is well worthwhile going right through the processes again. There will very seldom be failure if you are both patient and persistent.

Other special finishes

Unusual finishes worth trying on single pieces – or, if you are courageous, on all items in a bedroom or sitting room – can turn inexpensive and possibly shabby furniture into something attractive and probably unique.

Clearly it would be wrong to finish something which has good quality unspoiled veneer or is made from solid wood. But some of these finishes work well on whitewood furniture and even on hardboard. Generally speaking, a surface which is already in a dark shade needs to be bleached as a preliminary (see page 11).

Antique bloom

This is a novelty finish to be used with some restraint, perhaps on an occasional chair or the frame around a reproduction of an old painting.

Paint the item with an ivory paint (better than white though not so easy to find). When dry apply artist's glazing compound in which is mixed a little raw umber, burnt raw sienna or lamp black, depending on whether a brown, reddish or grey tone is desired. As soon as the glossy appearance begins to fade wipe away here and there to suggest parts which have aged. Protect the glazing with a coat of clear shellac or transparent varnish.

Artificial grain

This is practicable only on surfaces which are without a readily visible grain, ie, whitewood. First apply a ground coat of stain in whatever shade is desired. Allow it to dry and glasspaper till absolutely smooth. Clean away all dust.

Graining colours, called scumbles, are oil colours dissolved so that they are almost transparent. If the selected shade is rather darker than desired a little turpentine can be added.

Two flat brushes are required – 2cm ($\frac{3}{4}$in) and 5cm (2in) wide. They must be new or very thoroughly cleaned to free them from every vestige of paint.

Apply a coat of scumble very thinly with the 2cm ($\frac{3}{4}$in) brush, working in only one direction. Then go over the area with the 5cm (2in) brush, again working in only one direction.

Before the scumble dries it has to be combed. There are graining combs

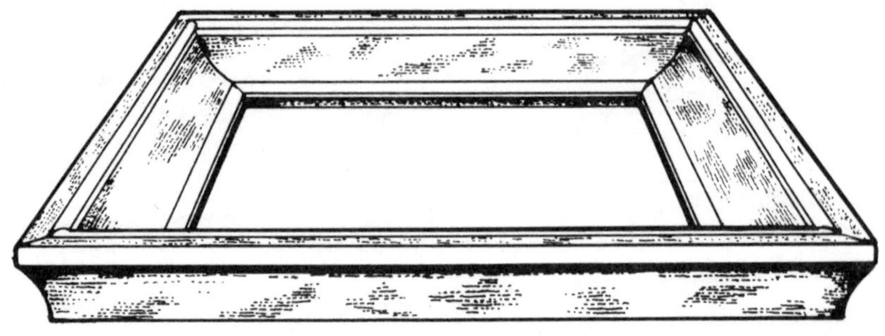

The antique finish is unusual and attractive, easily achieved with a little practice on a spare piece of wood

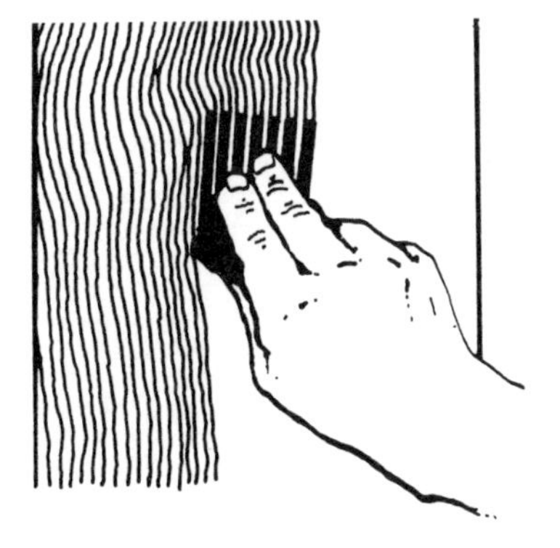

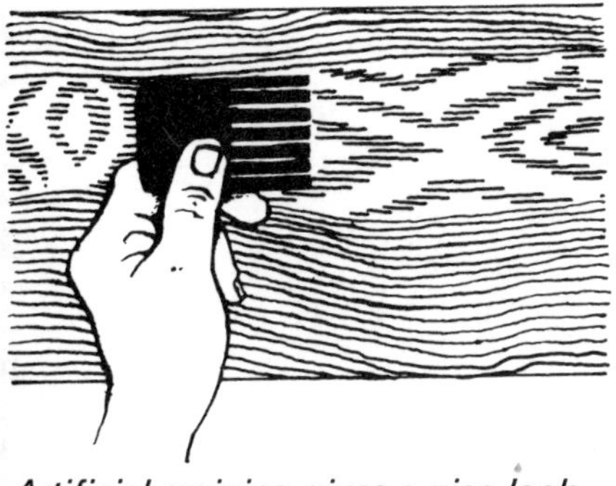

Artificial graining gives a nice look to cheaper woods

of various sizes. The teeth are of steel, so the expense of special combs can be avoided by using any metal comb. If, as is usual, the comb has one half of its width with widely spaced teeth and the other with the teeth closer together, it can be cut in half to provide two combs. Good results can also be achieved by cutting notches in a piece of thin, hard plastic, and glasspapering the points to ensure they are sharp and even.

The comb is held at an angle of 40° and drawn from one side to the other, rapidly but in a slightly wavering line. The teeth will remove most or all of the scumble, and the comb must be wiped clean after each stroke across the wood. It may well be that one comb produces all the graining effect desired, but usually it is best to use the wide-toothed comb first and then go over the area a second time with the fine-toothed comb, this time pressing more lightly.

The lines made by the combs may appear too sharp. They can be made to look more natural by taking a dry 5cm (2in) brush and, holding it upright, dab lightly over those lines which appear harsh. This process must be done immediately after combing and while the scumble is still wet.

After the surface is really dry go over it lightly with a piece of fine glasspaper, the surface of which has been made less abrasive by rubbing it against another piece of glasspaper of the same grade.

Brush away all debris meticulously and apply a coat of varnish. Copal oak varnish is suitable for dark finishes, transparent varnish for light finishes.

Blond

To produce a light-coloured finish, known in the trade as blond but actually pale gold, the surface of the wood must be removed to get rid of any stains, varnishes or paints, using an appropriate stripper. After washing with warm water apply household bleach, washing it away with hot water once the desired lack of colour has been obtained (this may need several applications of bleach).

Leave the piece to dry. Glasspaper until perfectly smooth and apply an amber-coloured stain. When dry lightly brush over a coat of shellac, followed by a coat of clear varnish. Rub lightly with fine glasspaper and give a second coat of clear varnish. The final step is to rub over with a pumice stone dipped in linseed oil.

Other special finishes

Blonding is really best restricted to close-grained woods. On open-grained woods a filler (see page 8) should be applied after the first coat of shellac and the surplus cleaned away. But filler may not be sufficient to conceal dark stains which may go right through the wood. No amount of bleaching or filler is likely to disguise such stains. It is, therefore, wise to make a test on some part of the furniture which will not be seen before attempting to blond open-grained wood.

Bone white

This finish is attractive for bedroom furniture of delicate appearance. It can be applied to open-grained woods because the attractive grain will show through the white surface.

After stripping to the natural surface and rubbing down, apply a coat of white enamel very sparingly, without any undercoat. Leave till dry and wipe on a coat of raw umber stain (it may be necessary to get a good hardware store to make this up for you; it consists of raw umber, which is dark yellow in colour, mixed with linseed oil and a drier). Leave for twenty to thirty minutes, watching for it to become tacky. Immediately wipe off the sticky surface.

This will leave lines along the grain which have a glistening appearance. Leave overnight to dry and then brush on a thin coat of shellac. When this is thoroughly dry polish with a silicone wax.

Shaded white

There are several tinges of colour which can soften the harshness of an item being painted white. Glasspaper the surface to provide a key and dust thoroughly. Suitable colours to mix with white paint are light blue, primrose, pink, or light green. The small tins of paint sold for touching up car bodies, etc., are an inexpensive source of this colouring additive. Experiment as to the amount required by pouring a little white paint on to a saucer and add a few drops of colour. Mix well and test on a piece of wood already painted white.

Silver-grey

This is a finish for oak, producing two tones. It will work only on solid oak, not imitations or veneers. After cleaning away all earlier finishes brush on black wood dye which has been dissolved in water. The proportion of dye to water is a matter of taste and experiments should be made on a spare piece of wood (which need not be oak).

When dry apply a filler (see page 8) mixed with an equivalent amount of white lead paste and turpentine. Allow the filler to set for about half an hour, and wipe off any excess across the grain of the wood. Leave to dry for twenty-four hours and then apply clear varnish, brushing first across the grain, and then, without replenishing the brush, with the grain. Leave to dry and repeat the two brushings of varnish. The unnaturally shiny look can be modified by rubbing over with a pumice stone dipped in linseed oil. When this is dry rub vigorously with a lint-free duster.

Two-tone

A finish to give two shades imitating oak, and eminently suitable for whitewood. Glasspaper to get a smooth finish and brush on oak stain, light or dark, according to preference. Leave to dry for about eight hours, and apply a thin coat of shellac. Leave to dry (about three hours) in warm dry conditions and brush on the same filler as for the silver-grey finish above. Leave to dry for twenty-four hours and then brush on varnish of the same shade as the stain used at the outset.

Varnish-stain

This finish virtually conceals the grain of the wood and is suitable if the grain pattern is unattractive or if a plain surface is desired.

Clean down to the natural wood, and then sponge over with turpentine to get rid of any grease or chemicals. Leave till thoroughly dry, then brush on varnish-stain. Several types are available, including those which are waterproof and unaffected by a considerable amount of heat. The only likely disappointment in giving a piece this finish is through using a coarse brush or applying the varnish too thickly. Two or even three coats, the previous coating rubbed down when dry, give an even colour and are less likely to wear away.

The gloss of varnish-stain, when new, is rather too marked for most tastes. It can be reduced to a pleasant sheen by going over the surface with a pumice stone dipped in linseed oil, and dusted when dry.

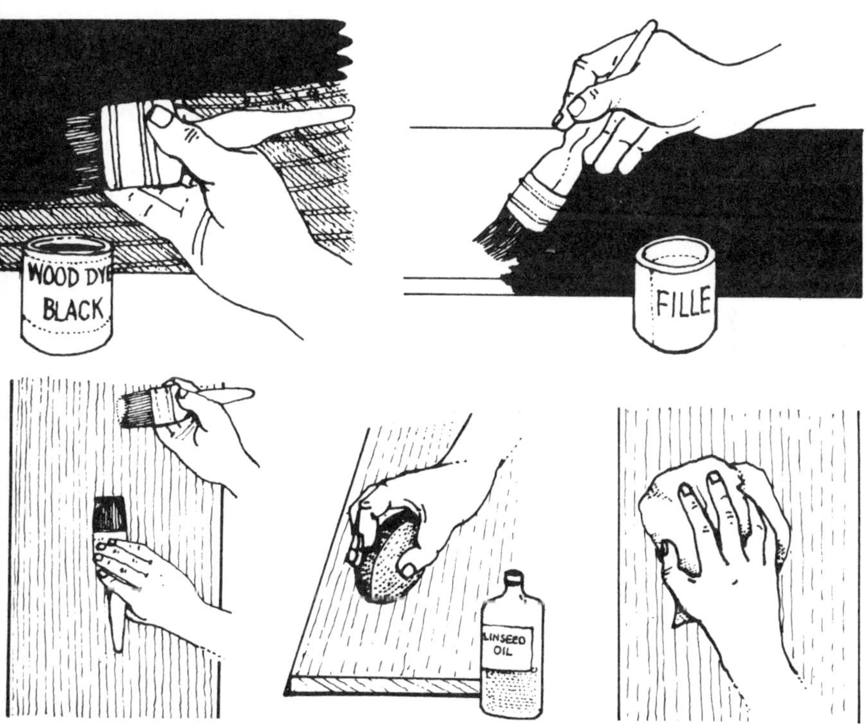

The silver-grey finish to be seen on antique oak can be produced on new timber with careful work, carried out in stages

Painted furniture

Probably the most attractive – and easiest – major change to make to the appearance of existing furniture is to paint it. Obviously it would be wrong to cover beautifully grained and fashioned wood of high quality. But many modern pieces, such as fitted wardrobes and dressing tables, cabinets, cupboards and chairs in bathrooms, and all wooden items in the kitchen, lend themselves to a colour scheme which can be extended to the fixed wooden items: doors, window frames, skirting boards, pelmets, etc.

The first objective is to prepare the surface thoroughly. Any existing varnish or paint must be removed with a stripper. Every vestige of the stripper and any remaining polish and grime should be dealt with by wiping with a rag soaked in white spirit, and then washed with warm water containing an ammonia-based detergent or liquid household ammonia.

The surface should be left until it is really dry and then gone over with fine glasspaper to deal with any traces of an earlier finish, roughened areas and swollen grain. The surface need not be glass smooth as it is essential to leave a key for the paint. But any dents, scratches or minor cracks and splits should be treated with filler (see page 8) and rubbed down. Finally, wipe with a lint-free duster to get rid of all debris.

Whatever some paint manufacturers may say all wood needs a primer. This is different from an undercoat. A primer produces the proper surface for the subsequent paint. An undercoat is to conceal a previous colour so that it does not show through the new colour. For softwoods the primer should be that for wood; for hardwoods it is better to use the more expensive aluminium wood primer. If you are not certain of the wood you are treating some manufacturers make all-surface primers which are an acceptable compromise.

When the primer is dry rub down lightly. If you have missed any scratches, old nail holes, etc, or if there are small spots caused by dust and grit, rub down once more and touch up with primer.

The work is now ready for the first of two undercoats. This should be of the shade advised by the manufacturers for the topcoat you have selected. If you have applied the undercoat properly and there are no runs (caused by charging the brush with too much paint and not brushing out evenly) there is no need to rub the undercoat with glasspaper.

Advertising makes much of the fact that only one coat of gloss topcoat is needed, and this is true enough on most items and with some paints. But if they are likely to be subjected to hard wear, as for instance in the kitchen or a children's playroom, a second coat applied now is better than having to deal with ugly blemishes and chips a few months later. When a second coat is applied the first one should be very lightly rubbed down.

As regards the actual painting technique you will, of course, have removed all handles and knobs. Use at least three brushes – 2cm, ($\frac{3}{4}$in) 3cm (1$\frac{1}{4}$in) and 5cm (2in) wide – the narrowest for tricky spots round keyholes, hinges, etc, the medium size for mouldings and narrow edges, and the large brush to cover flat areas.

In portable items such as chairs paint the underside first, then work from the top downwards. On large flat, vertical areas work from the top in an area not larger than 20cm (8in) square. Charge the large brush fairly generously and brush from right to left with vertical strokes, then (without replenishing the brush) with horizontal strokes. Finally brush lightly both vertically and horizontally until the brush slides over the surface and brush marks become invisible.

Do not work for an even line to the side and bottom against the areas still to be painted, and check that the paint has not ridged at the end of these brushings.

Repeat to the left of the painted area (if the job is so wide that the first painting has not gone from one side to the other) and then continue with 20cm (8in) square areas below. After the first area make the first series of vertical strokes upwards, decreasing the pressure as the brush reaches the edge of the painted area; then there is no risk of making a thick double coat at the join.

Incidentally, the non-drip jelly (thixotropic) paints, which are the principal ones for which one-coat use is advised, should be more generously loaded on the brush than with ordinary paints, and the third phase of brushing out should be kept to a minimum, or the coating will be pulled out too far and there may be patchiness, with no chance of remedying it with rubbing down for a second coat.

The second coat with fluid paints is applied in the same way, but the size of the rectangles should be slightly varied so that there is no risk of thickening at the edges, when a chessboard effect results.

When painting large vertical areas, work from the top from right to left using vertical strokes, then horizontal, finally in both directions until brush marks are no longer visible

Stencil and transfer decoration

The question of decorating furniture with a contrasting colour or colours needs to be carefully considered. Generally speaking, it would be regrettable to spoil the immaculate appearance of good quality natural wood with even minor touches of colour.

But wood which has been painted because it has little character, as in the case of whitewood pieces in bathroom, bedroom or kitchen, can be given a stamp of individuality provided the coloured pattern is restrained. A pretty border around doors and drawers on white painted items in the bedroom, for example, will minimise the suggestion of almost clinical austerity. In a child's bedroom or playroom appropriate designs will be attractive both to child and parents.

Generally speaking, coloured decoration should only appear on painted furniture. Apart from a white background, there are possibilities in a black background with vivid reds and golds. Just how effective this scheme can be may be seen in examples of old Russian and Eastern European furniture and, of course, in Chinese and Japanese work.

Two methods are available : stencils or transfers. Both are easier to use than might be envisaged. Stencil plates can be purchased in a great variety of designs and, provided they are cleaned after each application, a plate will last for thirty or more applications, allowing the design to be repeated as a border or on several pieces.

Stencils

Stencilling enthusiasts like to cut their own stencils, and anyone with some artistic talent – or the ability to copy a design accurately – can make perfectly acceptable stencils, cut from the specially prepared paper sold in art shops. If the stencil is to be used many times it is advisable to coat each side with shellac after the design has been cut out.

The materials required for stencilling on wood are oil colours in tubes, a small sheet of glass on which to mix the colour, a round short-bristled brush, white spirit, and cleaning cloths.

The surface to be decorated must be placed horizontally. In the case of chairs, small cabinets and cupboards they can be laid on a table. Doors of wardrobes, etc, will have to be removed.

A stencil applied to a chair

Make sure the area to be stencilled is dust-free. Squeeze out the oil colour on to the sheet of glass and work with a sliver of wood to a creamy, even consistency. If the colour is not precisely that desired and you are mixing colours prepare a generous amount so that there is no risk of having to make a second mix which will almost certainly not turn out to be exactly the same.

Measure the position for the stencil with extreme care, making very light guide marks with a soft pencil. Place the stencil in position and fix with cellulose tape, making sure that there is no bulge in the centre away from the edges.

First charge the brush quite generously with paint and then dab it on a cloth to get rid of any surplus; apply the colour while holding the brush vertically, dabbing rather than brushing. It does not matter how much paint you get on the upper surface of the stencil and going a little beyond the edges of the design will ensure that the result does not have a ragged outline. Peel away the cellulose tape while holding the stencil firmly and then lift it off quickly. Immediately clean the stencil with white spirit and wipe as dry as possible before repeating the process. Leave for twelve hours and then brush on a clear varnish.

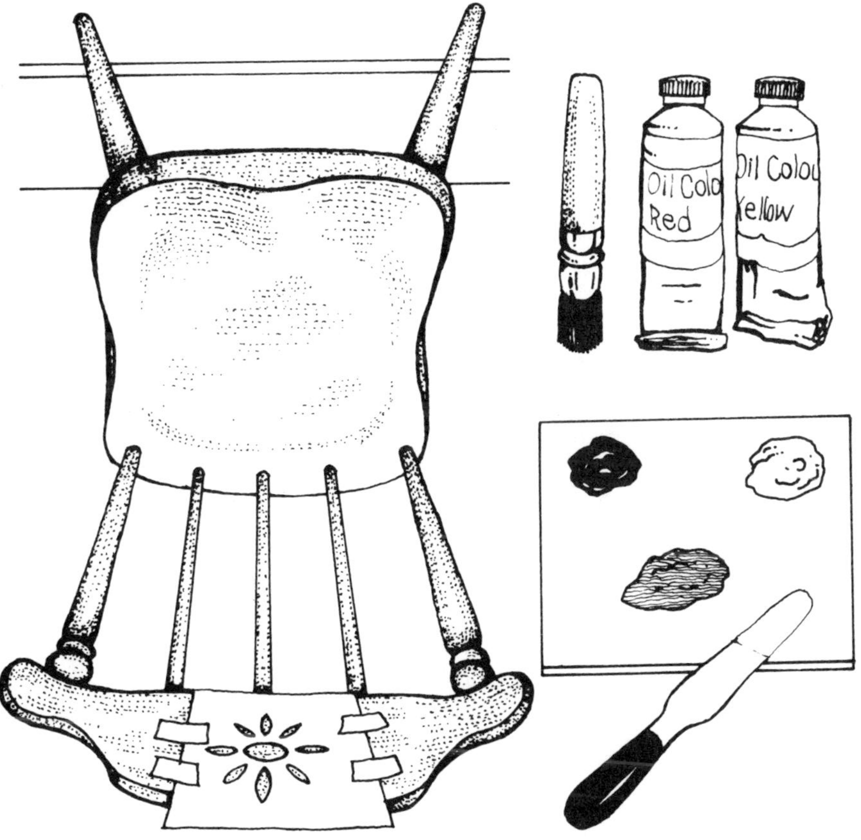

Materials necessary for applying a stencil. The area being decorated should be kept horizontal

Stencil and transfer decoration

Transfers

Transfers are excellent; they adhere firmly and will not peel, even with hard use as on the back rest of a chair.

They are printed in oil colours on specially prepared paper which is fairly thick and opaque, but usually an outline of the design is printed on the back for accurate positioning.

Several forms of fixative are offered by the makers. The established one is to coat the transfer with gold size or colourless oil varnish. This is applied with an artist's brush, not too lavishly and with care to ensure that every part of the design is covered but without going over the edges too much.

Now comes the only difficult part. The coated transfer must be left until the fixative is tacky – it feels sticky but none adheres to a finger lightly pressed on it. With gold size this will

Many transfers suitable for children's furniture are available

take between thirty and sixty minutes. With varnish it will be necessary to check at intervals for anything from two to six hours, depending on the temperature and atmosphere of the room.

Patience is necessary while waiting for this vital moment of the right amount of tackiness. Too dry and the transfer will fail to adhere; too wet and it will wrinkle and possibly tear when the backing paper is removed. As a final check lightly draw the knuckle of your forefinger across the surface. If it does not stick and there is a squeaking noise the tackiness is just right.

Lift the transfer from one end, turn it over and lower it into position. This must be done accurately at the first attempt, as there is not much chance of shifting it about once it touches the wood.

With a soft rag gathered into a ball rub vigorously all over the paper backing, working from the centre outwards to ensure that no air bubbles are trapped.

Next rub over the paper with a soft damp sponge, pressing firmly to help the paper absorb the water. Dampen the sponge frequently until the paper is well soaked. This will take about five minutes. Gently lift one corner to see if the transfer is adhering. If any colour remains on the paper it has not been wetted sufficiently. Smooth the corner down again and continue with the sponging.

With the papor removed, very gently wipe over the design with a sponge dipped in warm water and squeezed out. This will remove the slightly sticky surface with which the transfer was held to the backing paper. Then wipe dry, preferably with a wash leather or, if unavailable, use a soft linen rag.

With the most meticulous application it is almost inevitable that some gold size or varnish has got beyond the edge of the design. Left there, it will remain as a rather dark outline beyond the edge of the design, a defect particularly undesirable on a white background. Rubbing carefully with a rag moistened with white spirit wrapped round the end of the forefinger will remove it.

Leave the transfer to harden for at least twenty-four hours. Then coat with colourless varnish. This protective cost is not always necessary as some transfers come already varnished. They are more expensive but save trouble and obviate the difficulty of varnishing to cover the design completely yet not going beyond the edge where it might show, unless the whole area of the item is varnished.

The above type of transfer is that generally preferred by professional cabinet makers and furniture restorers, and has therefore been described in some detail.

But it should be emphasized that newer and purportedly easier types of transfer are worth considering. Self-fixing transfers, needing no gold size or varnish, are fixed either by heat (not really practical on furniture) or by a preparation already on the face of the transfer. It is first moistened with methylated spirit, allowed to reach the tacky stage, and then pressed down, the backing paper being removed by sponging as in the procedure already outlined. After the backing paper has been removed the transfer is allowed to dry for twenty-four hours and is then varnished or polished.

Dowels and tenons

Apart from dovetails, which are difficult for anyone but a trained carpenter to make or replace, the usual way to join one piece of wood to another in a typical piece of furniture is by a dowel or tenon.

A dowel is simply a small cylinder of wood which is inserted into holes in the adjacent pieces to be joined. Oak or beech is usually used, but any hardwood is suitable, the main consideration being that the dowel should not shrink with age.

Dowels are sold in many diameters and lengths. Their surface is smooth, and before use they should be given a serrated surface by pulling them through the jaws of firmly held pliers. This will increase the adhesion of the glue when the dowel is inserted.

In repair work the initial task is to remove the dowel which has snapped, leaving the rest of it in the two holes of the pieces which it used to hold together. This will mean drilling into the holes until all traces of the broken dowel have been removed. To obtain a close fit it may be necessary to increase the diameter of the hole slightly and to buy a dowel a little larger than the original. It will help to get the dowel well seated by very slightly tapering it at each end.

Coat one half of the dowel with glue and push home, hammering gently if necessary. Then coat the

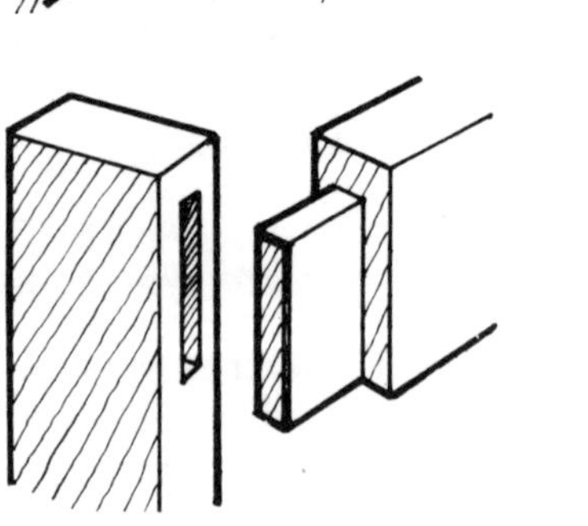

Typical dowelled joints and a tenon joint

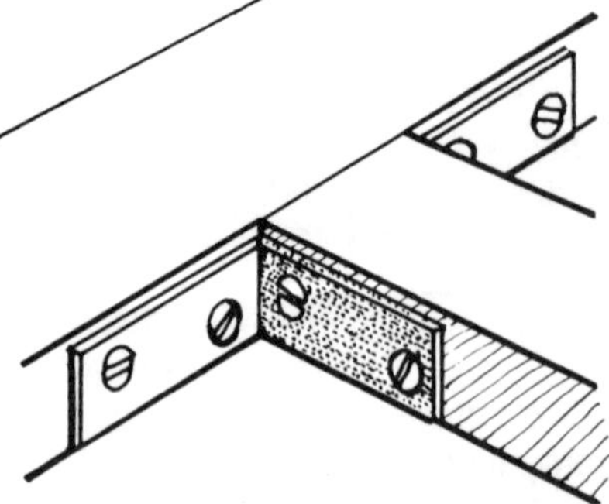

Metal angle brackets give a strong joint. Preferably use them in a concealed area

still exposed half and fit the other piece of wood over it, hammering until the edges of each piece meet. Additional strength can be achieved by applying a thin coat of glue to the area of wood around the dowel which will be covered by the end of the second piece of wood.

A tenon consists of a rectangular tongue of wood left in the centre of a length of timber when the rest has been cut away. The tongue fits exactly into a rectangular hole (or mortise) in the wood to be joined. Both tenon and mortise have to be very accurately cut, involving gauges and special tools. The job belongs to manufacture rather than repair.

A joint where a tenon and mortise have been used can become faulty either through loosening because of shrinkage and strain, or because the tenon has broken off.

In the first case all that may be needed is to take the two pieces of wood apart, clean away the old glue, liberally coat both tenon and mortise hole with glue and reassemble, holding together with clamps or several layers of cellulose tape. If shrinkage is clearly visible, a thin layer of plastic wood smeared on the sides of the mortise hole with a thin-bladed knife will help. Leave to dry, smooth away surplus with a file, glue, and reassemble.

When one side of the two pieces of wood held by the faulty tenon is not readily seen when the furniture is in use a small metal angle bracket screwed above or below the tenon will ensure a rigid joint and strengthen the re-glued tenon and mortise.

If the tenon has broken the remains in the mortise will have to be drilled out and the surplus of the tenon on the other side cut away and the surface smoothed. Fill the mortise with a piece of wood cut to fit and glued in. Then use the dowel idea, making the hole above, below or to the side of the removed tenon and mortise. This will not produce as strong a joint as the tenon but should give a reasonably robust joint if the surfaces of the two pieces are also glued. For additional strength add a metal angle bracket.

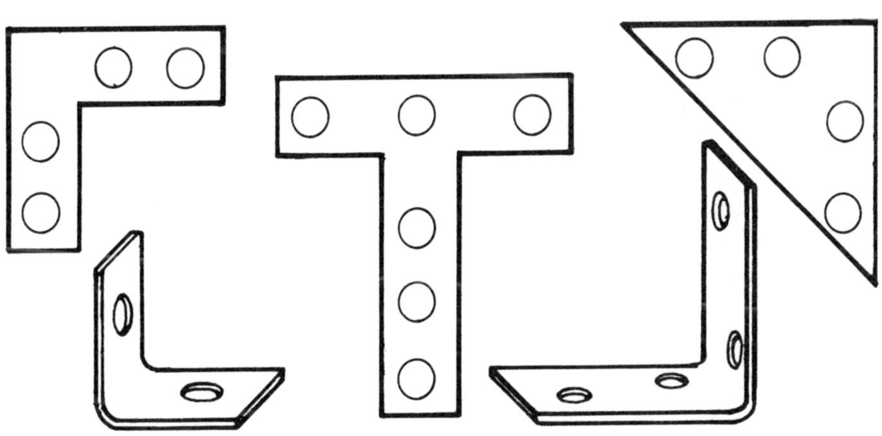

Typical metal angle brackets, all available in different sizes

Dowels and tenons

Makers of modern adhesives claim that their product will produce a bond stronger than the pieces of wood it joins. There is justification for this claim, and if the break of the tenon has not resulted in any slivers of timber falling away, and the broken ends fit like a perfect jigsaw then simply applying one of these strong adhesives may work. But it is essential that the two pieces be held immovable and without any strain for some time after joining, even with the instant contact adhesives. Again, it will do no harm to add additional strength with a metal angle bracket if it can be fixed without spoiling the appearance of the furniture.

In some T and L joints screws may have been used, especially if an earlier attempt has been made to repair or strengthen the joint. It is probable that the screw has been countersunk and the head concealed with filler or painted over. This concealment will have to be scraped away and the head of the screw cleaned in order to give a screwdriver a good grip. Unfortunately it is almost certain that the screw has rusted.

It may even have been unwisely given a coating of glue with the object of making a secure fix. A few drops of rust removing fluid or sewing machine oil rubbed around the screw head may help to loosen it if left for an hour to soak in.

Always use the correct size of screwdriver for the screw head when using strong pressure to turn it. Too narrow or thin a driver will almost certainly widen the slot or actually break it off.

If all attempts fail to move the screw with a screwdriver there is the heat method. Heat an old screwdriver until the metal is dull red and press the point against the screw, holding it there until the metal cools. The heat will have spread to the screw and caused it to expand. When it cools and contracts it should be looser.

A last resort is carefully to chisel away around the screw to make enough room to use narrow pliers held vertically. Here again, if the body of the screw is tightly embedded in the wood the head may break off. Then it will be necessary to drill down with a narrow gauge drill around the screw until it is freed. The hole will have to be filled with a piece of glued dowel and the surface finished off with plastic wood.

A dowel is the best method of restoring the joint. But if a screw is to be used it should be in a slightly different position from that of the previous screw, or failing that, of a larger gauge. Use brass or chromium-finished screws to ensure that there will be no difficulty in the future in removing them through rusting.

Light machine oil will usually loosen an obstinate screw if left to soak in

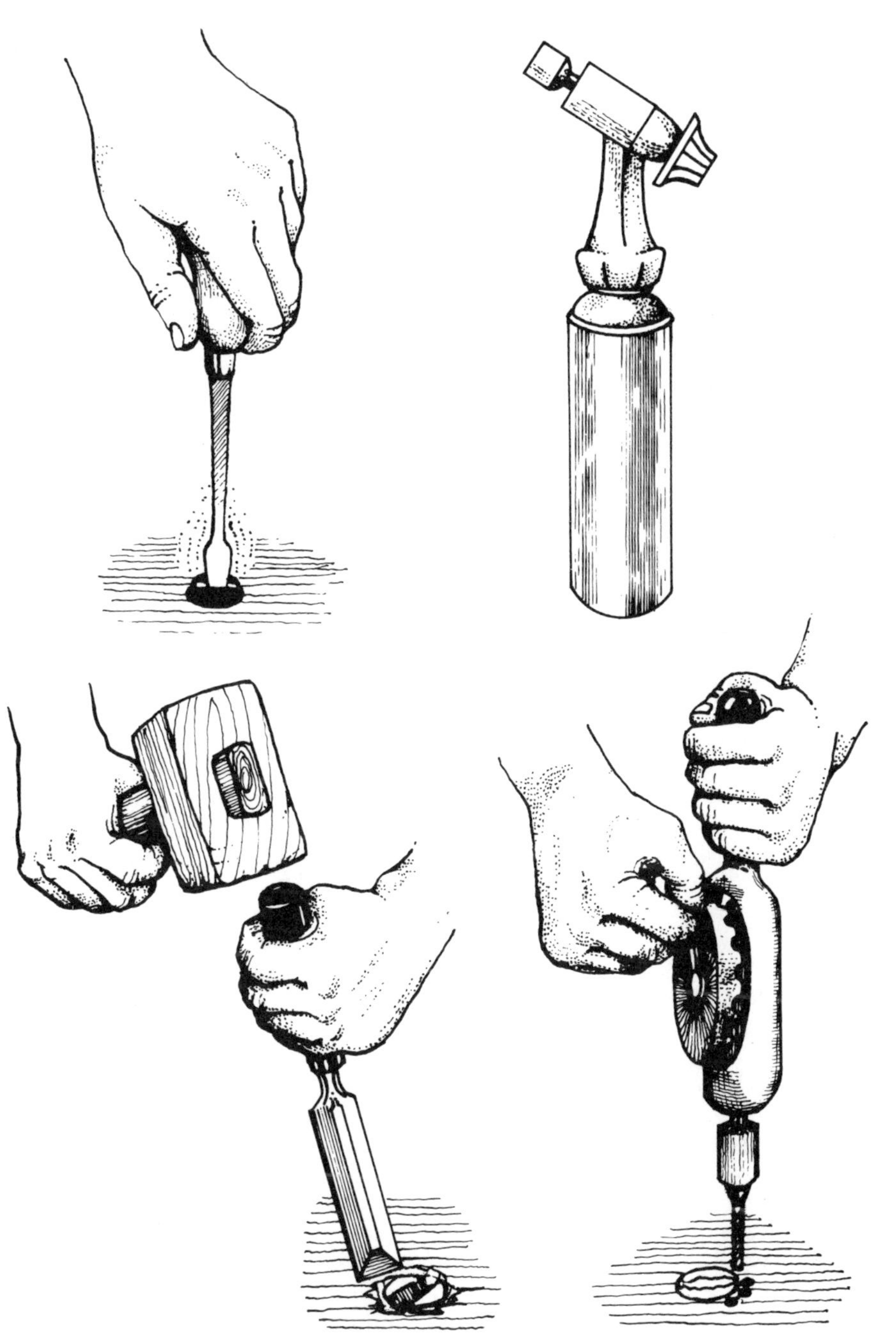

Other methods of loosening screws

Drawers

In very few homes do all the wooden drawers move inwards and outwards perfectly. There really is no need to put up with the jammed drawer, the one which slides past the surrounding edge, or gets askew if not adjusted as it is closed.

One may well regret that mass production, unseasoned wood, and other inefficiencies of modern manufacture seem inevitably to cause these defects. It is all the more exasperating when watching a TV programme on antiques or the work of famous cabinet-makers of the past to see how perfectly every drawer fits and moves. But in fairness to the modern maker, it must be remembered that these antique pieces were the work of masters of their craft. Probably the usual run of furniture in the past, now long since worn out and destroyed, was just as liable to faults.

But still there is no need to put up with this sort of annoyance. If a drawer is really stuck when closed heaving on it violently will merely make things worse and probably distort the rest of the construction. It is usually quite easy to remove the back and push the drawer outwards when there will be less stress and strain.

Before making any major repair try rubbing the runners with french chalk, and if that does not work, apply some silicone furniture polish, well rubbed in. Polish is far better than soap which quickly hardens and breaks up.

A common cause of a jammed drawer is damp. The wood swells because the moisture easily penetrates the untreated wood of the interior of the furniture. Aside from the obvious solution of seeing that the cabinet or chest of drawers is not subject to moist air from a nearby open window, steam in bathroom or kitchen and so on, it may be necessary to remove a slight amount of the surface at the top and bottom of the sides of the drawer or the runners.

Empty the drawer of its contents and find out at which point it is jamming. In the worst cases it may be necessary to plane away a little wood but in the majority of instances rubbing with glasspaper wrapped round a block of wood will do the job. The merest fraction needs to be removed to make all the difference.

Quite often the understandable belief that the drawer fits too tightly and therefore jams is in fact wrong. Indeed, wear and shrinkage may mean that there is a certain amount of play so that the drawer does not slide on a true parallel with the runners.

Remove the drawer and check the dovetails which join the sides to the front. If they have loosened then the sides will have moved outwards, thus scraping against the runners.

Unless the dovetails are really loose – in which case the best remedy is to take the drawer to pieces and re-glue it – a little adhesive can be worked into the gaps in the dovetails. As soon as it is tacky take a block of wood, hold it over the dovetails and tap with a hammer, first with the drawer on its end and then on its side.

Another cause of a drawer jamming is that the bottom edges of the sides have become worn. The drawer then drops and scrapes against the stops on the rail. The only solution is to cut away the sides at the bottom of the drawer, glasspaper to smoothness,

Faults needing repair include loose dovetails, worn runners and a warped, broken base—all common causes of jamming or sticking

and glue on new strips of wood to restore the correct depth of the sides. This job is not so difficult as it may sound. The essential is absolute accuracy of measurement.

Yet another source of jamming is that heavy and tightly-packed items have caused the bottom of the drawer to bend downwards or become loose. Usually there is a small overlap of wood at the back to allow for shrinkage and this can be tapped forward. If the sides have shrunk or a gap has appeared through warping the easiest way to remedy the trouble, short of replacing the base with plywood (which does not shrink) is to glue a thin strip of softwood across the underside.

Lastly, when a drawer closes too far inwards and ends up askew, the reason is invariably that the stop at the back has broken or become badly worn. Cut a piece of wood to the same size as an undamaged stop, remove the defective one, and fix the replacement with glue and panel pins.

Doors, chairs and tables

Doors

On all but very large and cheaply made doors on cabinets, wardrobes and cupboards it is unlikely that the wood of a sagging door itself has become distorted. The usual trouble is that the hinges were badly fixed at the outset or have become loose.

Unscrew the door at the hinges and remove them altogether. Check that the recess for the hinge plates is, in all instances, smooth and level, and takes the hinge so that its surface exactly matches the level of the surrounding wood. If it extends above that level, chisel or glasspaper the surface until the right depth is obtained. If the hinge is below the wood surface fix a piece of veneer or thin plywood in the recess.

Whichever is the fault fill all the old screw holes with plastic wood, allow to dry and replace the hinges, first on the door furniture, and then on the frame. Be sure to get the hinges absolutely level in the recess. When fixing on the door have assistance to hold it in position. Do not screw the hinges completely tight until the top and bottom of the door are parallel with the aperture.

Chairs

Uneven chair legs are a familiar fault. The end of one or two legs may have worn down, or the tenon joint at the top of the leg and the seat frame may have become loose.

The usual height for the seat of an upright chair is 44–46cm (17–18in), so a shortening of the legs by 1cm ($\frac{1}{2}$in) will not affect a comfortable seat. To check the length of all four

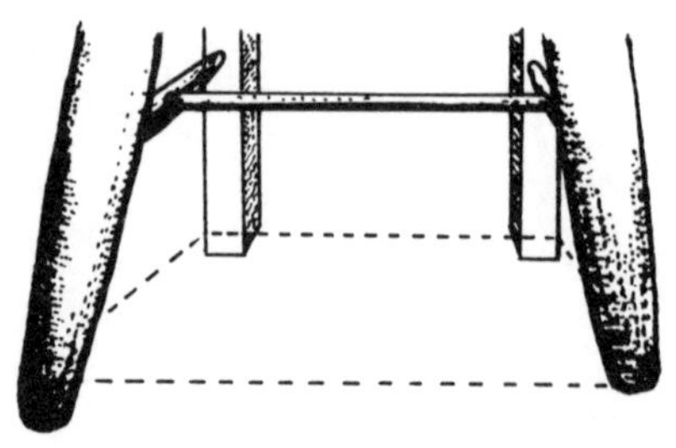

Check the lengths of the legs of a wobbly chair

legs place the chair on an absolutely flat table and rock it to ascertain which leg is too short. Its length determines the amount of wood to be cut from the other legs, checking first that any ferrule or glide fixed to the foot of the legs is not responsible for the discrepancy. The trouble is often caused by these fixtures becoming loose. They are either screwed in or have a press fit; in either case it is easy to remove them. Fill the screw or press hole with plastic wood, allow it to dry, and replace the ferrules, tapping them to the wood leg with a block of wood between ferrule and hammer.

Sometimes, however, one leg is clearly too short. Measure the gap when the other three legs are touching the table and mark this length on each leg. Saw away below the line and then glasspaper away the surplus, checking that all three legs are being rubbed down equally.

If the trouble is at the top of a shortened leg, remove any tie rails by twisting and pulling, and then do the same to pull the leg away. Clean off the old glue and put some plastic wood or a sliver of plywood into the base of the aperture, pushing it well

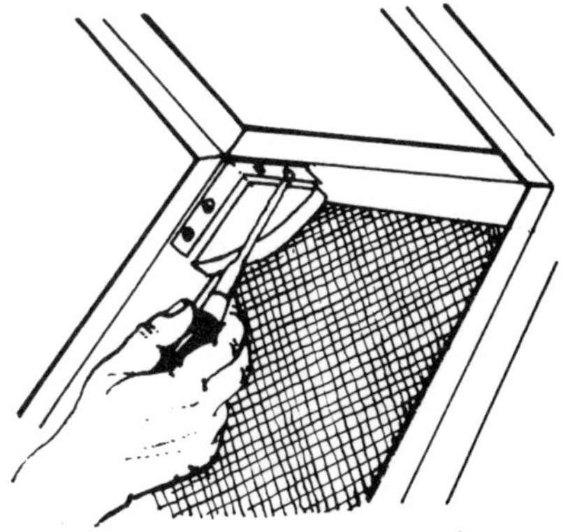

An unsteady chair can be repaired by dealing with the corner braces

down. Put the leg back temporarily to check that the length is now correct. Smear the top of the leg and the hole with glue and press home firmly, at the same time re-glueing the tie rails.

When a leg is actually broken it is best to replace all four legs with new ones, available in a huge variety of sizes and styles. The repair of a broken leg is rarely satisfactory. The stresses to which it is put in use are so great that any but an expert repair will result in another fracture.

A chair which becomes unsteady through loosening of the seat frame or back will usually be found to be faulty because the braces used to support the seat and keep the joints rigid have loosened. These braces will be seen by turning the chair upside down. They are against the seat frame at each corner. Invariably they are pieces of wood fixed with a couple of screws. Remove them, clean off any glue, fill the screw holes with plastic wood, allow it to dry and then re-glue and insert new screws, preferably of one size larger (but not longer) than the original screws. For extra strength screw on a small metal angle bracket below the brace.

Chair backs of the Windsor type often have loose rails and back rest. Repair is a simple matter of carefully removing the back rest and then the rails, cleaning off the old glue, re-glueing and reassembling. If a rail has broken, usually at either end, it will be necessary to drill out the stumps, making sure you remove all surplus wood. New rails are readily available, but may not be of the precise length. Buy a rail rather longer than required, match against a rail which is un-damaged and cut to fit. Make a test assembly, then glue the end holes and rail ends and tap them all together.

Tables

A wobbling occasional table or coffee table rarely needs to have its legs cut. The trouble usually is that the glue in the hole fixing the legs to the top, or the tenons, or the braces have be-come loose. Remove the legs and clean up any screw holes or joints, in the latter case sticking thin ply to the surfaces if the wood is rough and needs glasspapering to a harder surface. Fill screw holes with plastic wood and reassemble, taking care to align all the legs correctly.

Mouldings

Decorative beading and moulding along edges and at corners can be damaged though wear or breakage. Minor damage can easily be repaired with plastic wood. Roughen the edges around the broken area a little to provide good adhesion for the plastic wood which should be moulded between the fingers and applied a little at a time and pressed well in. Make the shape slightly larger and leave till completely dry, then rub down, first with a coarse glass-paper, finishing off with the finest grade available. Apply matching stain (if the plastic wood is not already coloured appropriately), rub with sandpaper again, check colour, apply more stain if necessary, and polish.

If the broken section is more than 4cm or 5cm ($1\frac{1}{2}$ or 2in) long it may be possible to buy a piece for replacement, for many mouldings and beadings are virtually standardized. If not, and the shape is not intricate, it is a comparatively easy job to make a replacement from softwood.

Cut a piece to the correct length but with the depth and width slightly larger. Stick this partly fabricated wood in position with a strong adhesive and leave till thoroughly dry.

By working from each side the silhouette can be followed with a chisel; be careful to leave the shaping overall larger than the adjacent moulding. With rounded file and glasspaper wrapped round a cylindrical piece of wood (eg, a section of broom handle) the exact shape of the moulding can, with patience, be achieved. Stain and again smooth with fine glasspaper, finishing off with a polish.

If the pattern of the moulding is intricate, or the broken area is extensive, it is simpler to remove it entirely and replace with a new piece. It may be rather difficult to remove the old piece, and care must be taken not to damage the adjacent wood. Clean away all vestiges of adhesive and remove any pins, nails or screws which may have been used to fix it. If an epoxy adhesive is used on the new moulding there will be no need to use panel pins or screws to ensure it is firmly fixed.

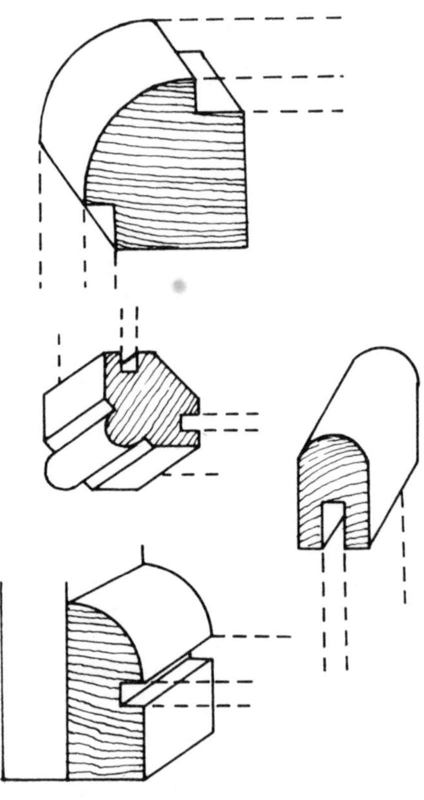

Mouldings are widely available in several sizes and shapes

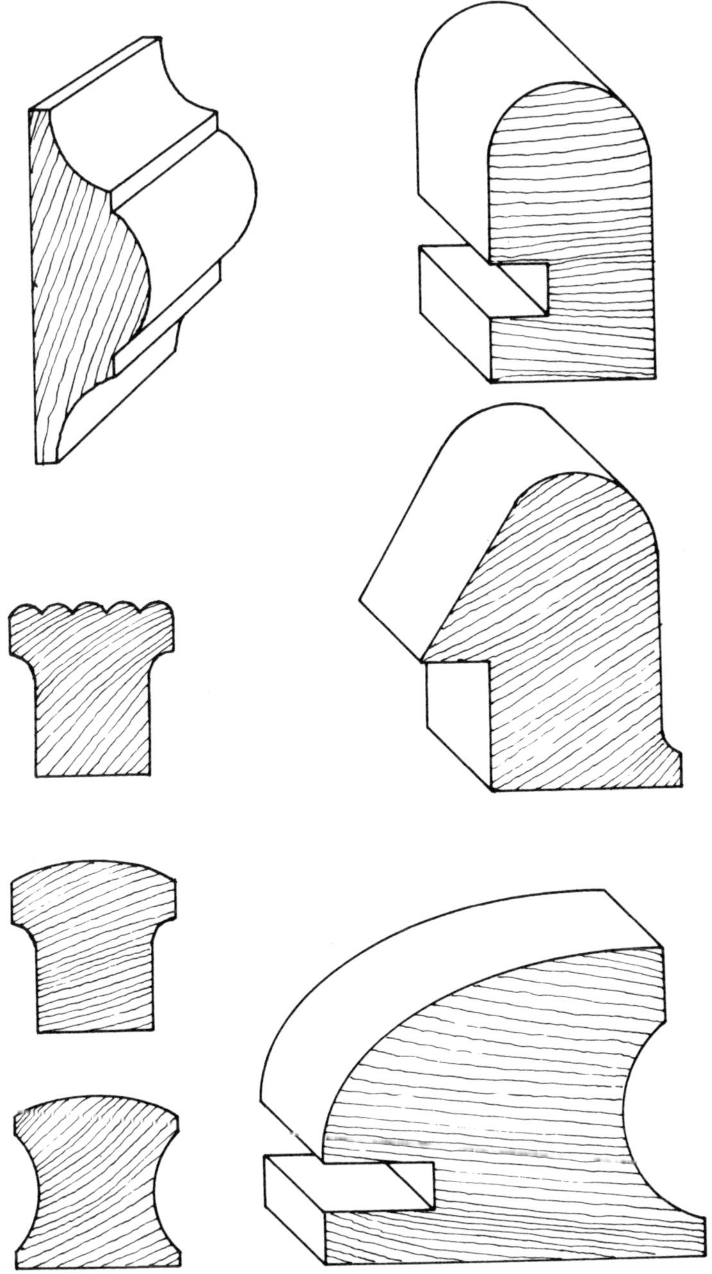

Veneers

A lot of modern furniture is finished with a veneer, allowing finishes to be in virtually any kind of attractive wood over a less expensive wood used in the basic construction of the piece.

There are various types of veneer. Face veneers are thin and mainly give a decorative finish. Constructional veneers are produced in various thicknesses in the same way as plywood, though not cross-laminated as plywood is; these veneers are widely used in the furniture industry. Because of their thickness they are not so likely to peel or chip. Pliable veneers, which are not true veneers, are available under a variety of trade names and are mainly for the amateur, since they are easy to cut. They are produced in a great variety of finishes. In buying a piece of veneer for a repair not only the colour, grain pattern and type of wood should be checked against a specimen from the damaged item, but also the thickness.

Modern adhesives are so efficient that only misuse, prolonged damp, or actual abrasions are likely to damage a veneer sufficiently for the basic wood to be exposed.

The most usual blemish is a bubble caused by trapped air underneath, usually the result of something hot being placed on the surface or, in older pieces, inefficient glueing. Attempting to press the bubble down with a piece of timber hit with a hammer or with a hot iron is futile, as the trapped air cannot escape. A small bubble may sometimes be dealt with by piercing the centre with a fine needle, warming the area with a hair dryer and then gently tapping with a hammer over several sheets of newspaper placed over the bubble to prevent denting.

More usually the air gap below the bubble means that the glue has long since dried to a skin and can no longer provide good adhesion. It is therefore necessary to introduce fresh glue. Cut into the bubble along a grain mark with the corner of a razor blade or a very thin sharp knife.

Lift each side of the slit by inserting a matchstick so as to provide just enough space to insert adhesive on the tip of a knife blade. Using a transparent adhesive, apply it beneath the veneer sparingly and evenly and immediately wipe away any that may have crept beyond the edge.

Press the veneer back, working from the edge of the bubble area and leaving the edges of the cut to the last so as to ensure that no air is trapped.

Finally, with two or three pieces of paper covering the area to avoid damaging the surface, tap lightly but repeatedly all over the area. So long as the original cut followed the line of grain and a thin blade was used the cut should be invisible.

Loose veneer

This invariably occurs at the edge of a surface. With care it can be lifted beyond the loosened area by inserting a flat, round-ended knife, and gently moving it from side to side; then you can penetrate a little further into the still attached area. The aim is to raise the veneer sufficiently to clean away the original glue on both the underside of the veneer and the surface of the wood base. This can be done with a sharp penknife if the veneer is bent upwards and kept up with a few slivers of wood. Ideally they should be tapered so that there is no risk of cracking the veneer in the area between the raised portion and the main part still stuck down.

When you are satisfied that the glue has been removed (any tenacious pieces can be smoothed down with fine glasspaper) smear PVA adhesive on both sides and press down.

It is essential that the treated area be cramped, with blocks of wood between the cramps both above and below the treated area to avoid damage; as an extra precaution place a sheet of polythene on the upper surface to ensure that any surplus or exuded adhesive does not bond the block to the veneered surface.

If cramps are not available or if the area does not lend itself to their use strap with tightly drawn cellulose tape and fix a weight above the area. Do not remove cramps or weight and tapes for at least six hours.

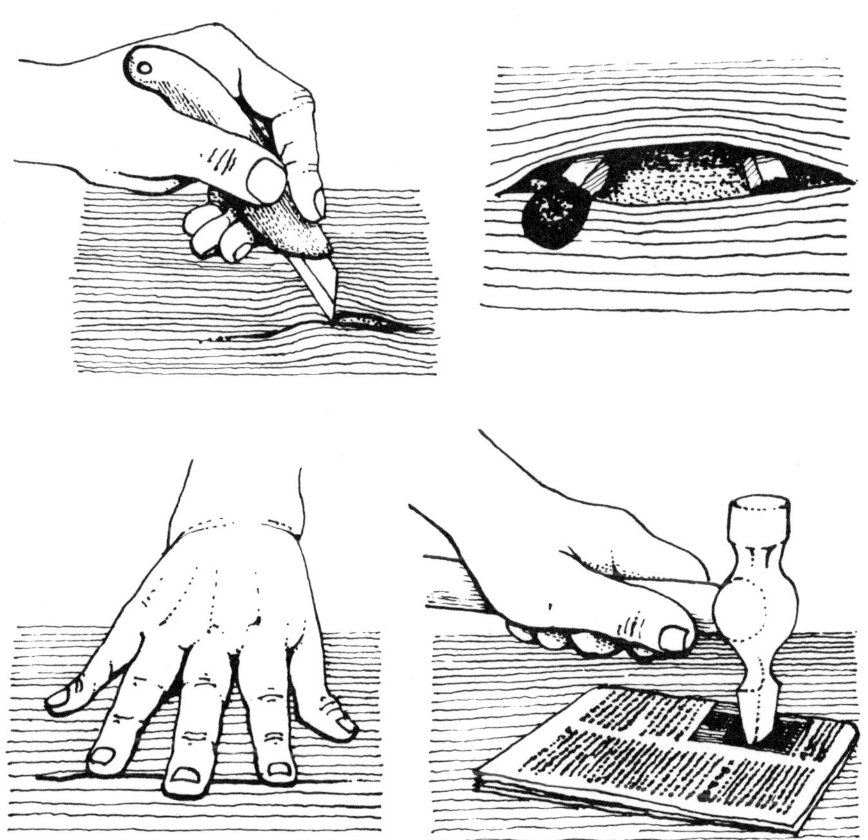

To remove a bubble from a veneered surface: cut along the grain, insert matchsticks each end of the slit, apply adhesive, remove matches and press down. Cover area with newspaper and tap lightly with a hammer

Veneers

Chipped veneer

A more difficult repair is where some veneer has been chipped or broken off completely. Very rarely will the broken part leave a neat break, so the first thing to do is to cut a little farther in, whenever possible following the marking of the grain. If this is impossible it is better to cut away at an acute angle rather than at a right angle.

Check that the undamaged veneer is still adhering; if a slight gap is evident stick down with adhesive, being careful to wipe away any surplus on the exposed wood.

The replacement veneer must obviously be of the same finish and colour, and with a grain pattern as close as possible to the original. Good DIY shops stock a great variety of veneers. Ideally you should take a scrap of your veneer with you to make a good match. In any event you must know what type of wood your veneer is. The type is really more important than exact colour, for it will be possible to change the colour with a dye. The dye must be generously applied at least three times so as to ensure that it soaks in and will not be removed by glasspapering. As you will have to buy a larger piece of veneer than you need you can experiment on spare pieces to find the appropriate hue from dyeing.

Clean up the edges of the undamaged veneer and then fix a sheet of tracing paper with cellulose tape over the area to be filled. Carefully trace the shape. Stick the tracing to the underside of the replacement veneer and go over the tracing with a sharp, hard pencil. With a sharp knife cut out the shape, making the cut on the outside of the line rather than through it. The small surplus will ensure a tight fit and any real excess can be removed with glasspaper.

After checking that the patch is an exact fit, that the graining makes a good match, and the thickness of the veneer is correct, go over the base wood with a piece of cotton wool soaked in methylated spirit to remove dust and any remaining glue. Apply contact adhesive thinly to both the veneer and the wood base. When touch-dry press down, starting from the centre and working to the edges. Leave to dry with a weight evenly covering the whole area. Then lightly glasspaper if the edges are not quite level. Remove all dust with methylated spirit and polish.

Laying veneer

When a veneer on the top of a small table, the face of a drawer or a shelf is very badly chipped and damaged, a completely new veneered surface can be the only feasible repair. A veneer can also be used to cover plain wood provided it is perfectly smooth and more than 2cm (¾in) thick.

After buying the desired kind and size of veneer place it on the area to be covered and mark out the shape with a surplus of about 2cm (¾in) all round. If more than one piece of veneer is being used allow this extra piece 2cm (¾in) extra width at the joint.

Generously dampen the sheet of veneer with cold water and place between two heavy, perfectly clean boards. If more than one sheet is to be used dampen them all and stack them together. They should be left for three or four hours by which time the moisture will have rendered them pliable.

Meantime score the surface to be veneered in order to provide a key. Brush over with Scotch glue and leave to dry. Whatever some dealers may claim, there is nothing better than Scotch glue for veneering, as it is water soluble.

When the veneer sheets are pliable apply another coat of Scotch glue to the wood surface and place the veneer in position. A veneer hammer is available in DIY stores, but a light wooden mallet or a hammer with its head protected in felt will serve.

Tap from the centre towards the edges to get rid of air bubbles, and use a slightly sideways motion rather than tapping vertically. Rub over with the fist as you proceed. This will enable you to check that there is no unevenness and the whole area of veneer is adhering strongly.

When laying more than one piece of veneer lay the subsequent leaf about 2cm ($\frac{3}{4}$in) over the one already stuck down. As soon as it has been firmly bonded cut away the surplus and then rub down with the mallet on each side to close the joint. Satisfied that the joint is almost invisible, cover it with a strip of strong brown paper adhesive tape, then a piece of clean paper and lastly a weight. Leave for an hour or so. Remove the tape and clean away any surplus glue at the joint with warm water.

Finally cut away the surplus round the edges, glasspapering to get a neat finish flush with the edge of the base.

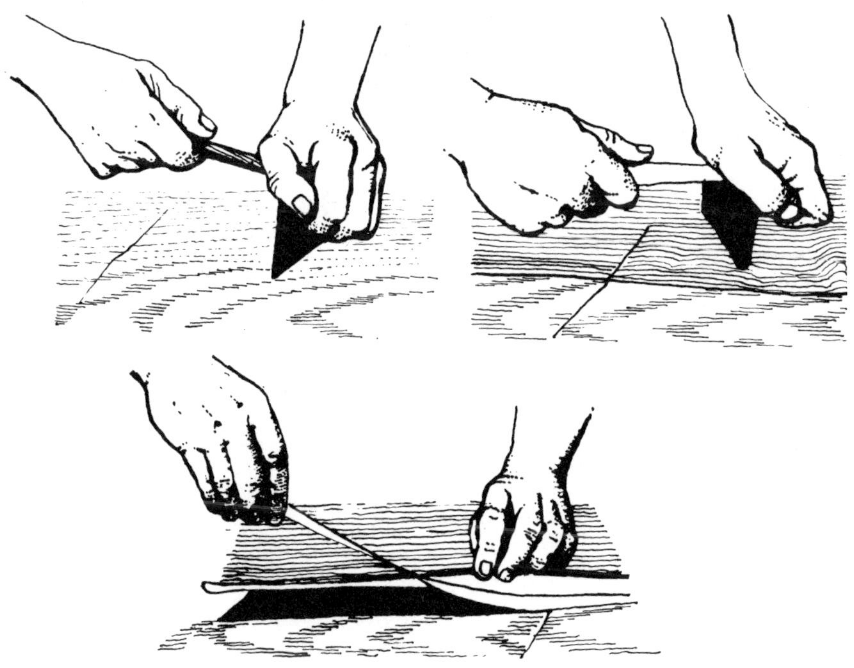

Laying veneer using a veneer hammer

Upholstered furniture

Repairing and replacing upholstery is a project only incidentally connected with work on the wood of furniture. As regards pieces such as easy chairs and sofas, where wood is merely a framework to support, renovation of the upholstery is a specialized craft and, on the whole, better left to an expert.

However, there are instances where upholstery is a minor part of the piece. Chairs with a loose seat and a padded back rest are an example.

In renovating such items the upholstered parts must usually be removed before any work is undertaken on the wooden frame. If the seat is padded remove the material carefully and keep it as the pattern for cutting out a new piece.

Check the exposed wooden frame for loose joints and woodworm, and deal with any defects.

If new padding is required it is easier to buy foam rubber (the high density kind) than to renew the horsehair or wadding. Replace the webbing no matter how good the original webbing appears to be. It is bound to have slackened. Cover the whole of the underside by tacking and sticking a piece of hessian on to it. This keeps out damp and dirt.

For the back of the chair follow the pattern of the original material, tack down on a thin coating of adhesive on the frame, and cover the tacks with braid. Precautions should be taken to pull the material as tight as one's strength allows so as to avoid slackening and creases in use. Four hands are better than two in getting the material tight on all sides.

Many chairs are upholstered in leather or a synthetic version of leather. In this case it is better not to remove the leather unless it is going to be replaced – a difficult and rather expensive job.

Greasy marks can be removed or at least lightened by gently rubbing in some fuller's earth, leaving for a time and then brushing away. If the stain is deep it may be worthwhile rubbing cautiously with a pad of cotton wool just slightly dampened with methylated spirit or a dry cleaning fluid. But do not soak the leather as it will make a ring round the stain.

General griminess and discoloration are best cleaned with a proprietary hide food or saddle soap. When treating the adjacent wood with stain, varnish or polish, beware of applying any of these liquids or substances close to the leather. It will discolour the edge. Stick a length of cellulose tape just over the edge of the leather, pressing it down securely.

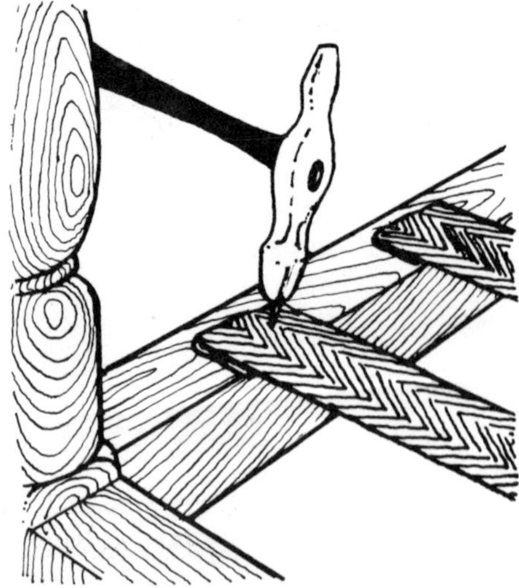

Always replace old webbing on upholstered seating, pulling each length tight

A cut-away section of a typical upholstered chair. When renewing the padding, high-density foam rubber is the best material to use

Bamboo repairs and cleaning

Chairs, stools and such small items as house plant stands made of bamboo are increasingly popular, especially for use in sun lounges and temporarily in the garden. If well made, as it usually is when imported from Asia, bamboo furniture lasts well despite the degree of flexibility of construction and the absence of connections in joints.

The usual reason for deterioration is a failure to keep out damp, for instance, leaving it unprotected on an open verandah during the winter, allowing dust and grease to collect between the lengths of cane and, paradoxically, causing the bamboo to become brittle if placed too near radiators and fires.

Bamboo furniture deserves regular dusting with a dry paint brush to reach between the canes. Better still is to vacuum clean with a brush attachment. Afterwards, application of a wax polish, used sparingly so that all the polish is thoroughly rubbed to a patina, will protect the surface and inhibit mould and rot.

In an annual spring clean it is worthwhile, on a sunny day, to wash bamboo pieces with tepid water containing washing up liquid and rinsing well to get rid of any trace of detergent. If the water seems to be repelled in some areas it indicates that earlier wax polish has created an over-thick skin. In this case go over the whole piece with a rag just dampened with methylated spirit. This will remove the grease. A glance at the rag will show that a lot of dirt has been removed as well.

If some lengths of bamboo have split or broken it is possible to replace them with a modicum of skill. A length of the right thickness can usually be obtained by searching around supplies in a garden shop if a local craft shop does not stock bamboo. After cutting to the required length let the cane soak in very hot water for thirty minutes when it will be quite easy to bend it to the desired shape. If possible use the original binding as it is difficult to buy – or for that matter to slice away a strip from a bamboo cane – to make a good match. Plastic imitations are available but they rarely have a real bamboo look.

Bear in mind that bamboo can be painted or varnished. This may wear away in places because of friction in what is basically a flexible construction, but an annual touch-up will remedy imperfections. The best method of getting an even, thin cover of paint reaching between the lengths of cane is to use an aerosol paint. Those sold for touching up car bodies are ideal. Give the piece at least two coats, allowing the first one to dry for an hour before spraying again.

There are no nails or screws in the joints of bamboo furniture. When binding is broken, it is best to remove and rewind, following a similar joint, and fixing the end with adhesive

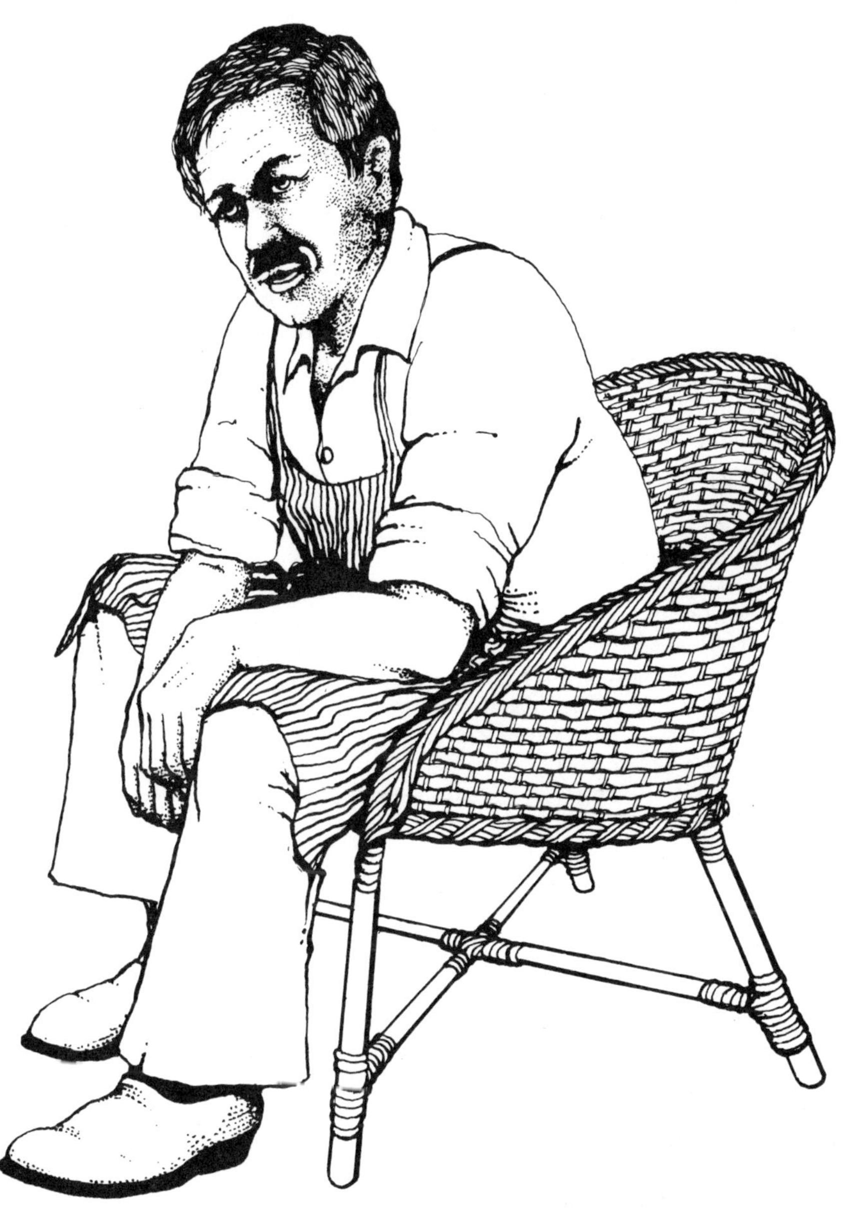

Woodworm

The woodworm or furniture beetle is one of the worst menaces affecting furniture; unfortunately the older the item and the better the wood the more vulnerable it is.

Evidence of the presence of woodworm is all too familiar: minute holes in the surface and a fine powder on the floor, with more powder dropping out if the affected area is tapped.

Most woods can be affected, the only exceptions being solid mahogany and teak.

Eradicating woodworm must be tackled over a long period, because its life cycle is at least three years. Eggs are laid in crevices in spring and early summer. The grubs, almost invisible to the naked eye, burrow into the wood and remain concealed for about two years, then they change into winged beetles and gnaw their way to the surface, producing the dust and the visible worm holes. The beetles immediately mate, and the cycle begins all over again. As the beetles can fly, previously unattacked pieces of furniture in the same room or house may be selected for the next batch of eggs.

The object of any treatment must be to kill the grubs hatched in early summer as they start to make their holes, and to wage prolonged war on those which are living well below the surface for month after month.

Insecticides sold to treat woodworm are completely effective when properly used. The newly hatched grubs on the surface will be killed if the liquid is sprayed or rubbed over the surface and into crevices and joints. Those already in their burrows will succumb only if the insecticide reaches them. This means using an aerosol or plastic container with an injector so that the liquid can be forced well into the holes. Merely putting a film of liquid over the hole will not be effective, and even accurate injection into the hole may not reach the grub through a screen of dust. Complete eradication is only certain if the treatment is repeated regularly, say every three months, and especially in March and April when the newly fledged beetles are moving outwards.

Some precautions in using an insecticide are advisable. Beware of applying it to the surface of light coloured wood without making a test on an area where possible staining will not matter. Be careful not to get the liquid on the skin; wear rubber gloves and burn any duster which has become impregnated. Avoid breathing the fumes, especially with an aerosol. Apply the liquid at arm's length with the windows open. Keep children and pets out of the room and cover any house plants with sheets of newspaper.

The marks of woodworm are clearly visible in this table leg

Useful addresses

As well as do-it-yourself shops and timber yards, arts and crafts shops are excellent sources of items not in wide demand. These shops are often more ready to ascertain names and addresses of specialist manufacturers, and order small quantities, than are the firms with a large trading turnover.

The following manufacturers and suppilers are merely a selection. They are mentioned as they offer explanatory literature and price lists direct to the public.

Garryson Abrasives Ltd, Spring Road, Ibstock, Leicester LE6 1LR	*Abrasives*
English Abrasives, Marsh Lane, Tottenham, London N17	*Abrasives*
Unibond Ltd, Tuscan Way, Camberley, Surrey GU15 3DD	*Adhesives*
Woodfit Ltd, Maxwell Road, Borehamwood, Herts	*Furniture fittings* (*catalogue 30p*)
J. Simble and Sons 76 Queen's Road, Watford, Herts	*Mail order for tools, etc.*
Wilcot Ltd, Fishponds, Bristol BS16 2BQ	*Paint removers*
Hobbies and Handicrafts Ltd, Elvin Road, Dereham, Norfolk NR19 2DX	*Stencils and transfers*
Ashley Iles Edge Tools Ltd, Woodcarver Works, Spilsby, Lincs	*Tools*
Skarsten Manufacturing Co. Ltd, Hydeway, Welwyn, Herts AL7 3AH	*Tools*
Stanley Tools Ltd, Woodside, Sheffield	*Tools*

Berman Bros. Ltd, Goodwin Road, Edmonton, London N9 0EP	*Veneers*
World of Wood Ltd, 2 Industrial Estate, Mildenhall, Suffolk	*Veneers*
Clam-Brunner Ltd, Maxwell Road, Borehamwood, Herts	*Woodfillers*
Roncraft, East Molesey, Surrey KT8 9BR	*Wood finishing products*
General Woodwork Supplies 76 High Street, Stoke Newington, London N16	*Wood cut to required size*
Furniglas Ltd, Birchwood Industrial Estate, Great North Road, Hatfield, Herts AL9 5JU	*Wood varnishes and dyes*

Further reading

Bateman, Robert *Victorian Furniture Transformed* (Stanley Paul, 1971)
Bausert, John *Complete Book of Wicker and Cane Furniture Making* (Drake Publications, USA, 1976)
Hayward, Charles *English Period Furniture* (Evans Bros, 1977)
——,—— *Practical Veneering* (Evans Bros, 1975)
——, ——*Teach Yourself Carpentry* (English Universities Press, 1977)
Molloy, E. (ed) *Newnes Practical Handyman* (2 vols) (Newnes, nd)
Pain, F. *The Practical Woodturner* (Evans Bros, 1957)
Shea, John G. *Antique Country Furniture of North America* (Evans Bros, 1976)
Taylor, Victor *Modern Furniture Construction* (Evans Bros, 1977)

Periodicals

Do It Yourself, Homemaker, Practical Woodworker, Woodworking. The last is available in bound form annually, and also issues various handbooks on all branches of carpentry. Details from Model and Allied Publications Ltd, PO Box 35, Bridge Street, Hemel Hempstead, Herts.

Special bookshops

The Bicester Book Shop, 5 Kingsley Road, Bicester, Oxon, specializes in books, both new and second-hand, on all branches of crafts connected with wood.
Woodcraft, 313 Montvale Avenue, Woburn, Mass. 01801, USA, has one of the world's largest stocks of craft books, as well as selling tools. Its catalogue is available at a nominal price. International reply coupon for enquiry about latest edition.

Illustrated by Robin Wiggins

British Library Cataloguing in Publication Data
Newell, John
Renovating furniture. – (Penny pinchers).
1. Furniture – Repairing
I. Title II. Series
749'.028 TT199

ISBN 0 7153 7868 6

Set in 9D on 11pt. Univers
and printed in Great Britain
by Redwood Burn Limited
Trowbridge & Esher
for David & Charles (Publishers) Limited
Brunel House Newton Abbot Devon